Collecting R...
Kewpies ®

AMERICAN KEWPIES

David O'Neill
Janet O'Neill Sullivan

Schiffer Publishing Ltd

4880 Lower Valley Road, Atglen, PA 19310 USA

Copyright © 2003 by David O'Neill and Janet O'Neill Sullivan
Library of Congress Control Number: 2003101970

Designed by Bonnie M. Hensley
Cover design by Bruce Waters
Type set in Seagull Hv BT/Aldine 721 BT

ISBN: 0-7643-1855-1
Printed in China
1 2 3 4

Published by Schiffer Publishing Ltd.
4880 Lower Valley Road
Atglen, PA 19310
Phone: (610) 593-1777; Fax: (610) 593-2002; E-mail: Info@schifferbooks.com
Please visit our web site catalog at www.schifferbooks.com
We are always looking for people to write books on new and related subjects. If you have an idea for a book, please contact us at the above address.

This book may be purchased from the publisher. Include $3.95 for shipping. Please try your bookstore first. You may write for a free catalog.

In Europe, Schiffer books are distributed by
Bushwood Books
6 Marksbury Avenue
Kew Gardens
Surrey TW9 4JF England
Phone: 44 (0) 20 8392 8585; Fax: 44 (0) 20 8392 9876; E-mail: Bushwd@aol.com
Free postage in the UK. Europe: air mail at cost.

Contents

Acknowledgments

Thank you seems insignificant in expressing our gratitude to the people who have helped to bring this book to fruition. A special thank you to those who have shared their wonderful collections and talents, which made this book possible: Judy Abshire, June Anderson, the Bonniebrook Historical Society, Jean Cantwell, Violet and Chick Fairbanks, Kathy and Don Feagans, Luther Gillett, Marguerite Jennell, Vernon and Marlys Jordan Jr., the Rose O'Neill Foundation, Viola and Elmer Reynolds, Karen Stewart-Salaz, Eleanor Waladkewics, Kathy Wales, and Susan Wilson.

Introduction

Rose Cecil O'Neill

Rose Cecil O'Neill, the second child of William Patrick and Asenath Cecelia, was born in Wilkes-Barre, Pennsylvania, on June 24, 1874. The family moved to Battle Creek, Nebraska, in 1876. At age fourteen, Rose won an art contest for a drawing by a Nebraska school child sponsored by the *Omaha World Herald*. This started her in a career of illustrating stories in pen and ink. By age seventeen, she was illustrating "Arabian Nights" for a Denver Magazine, *The Great Divide*. By age nineteen, Rose had written a novel, *Callista*, with sixty-three illustrations. She took it and other drawings and headed for New York, stopping in Chicago to visit the 1893 World's Fair, where she saw her first modern paintings and sculptures.

Advised by a publisher to wait until she was older to write (though he did encourage her to continue drawing), Rose lodged at the Convent of the Sisters of St. Regis in New York City where she studied . . . and began creating illustrations for *Truth, Collier's Weekly, Harper's Monthly, Weekly, Puck, New York Life, Brooklyn Life,* and *Bazaar*. Two nuns would accompany Rose on visits to editors. She made drawings for a smart Chicago publication, *Art in Dress*.

In 1896, Rose married Gray Lathan and began signing her drawings, O'Neill Lathan. Gray had no idea of "mine and thine" in the matter of money, however. He would go to offices and collect before Rose could get the drawings done, and leave her penniless. Rose subsequently retreated to her beloved Bonniebrook, the O'Neill family home in the hills near Branson, Missouri, and obtained a divorce.

Rose relaxing at Bonniebrook.

At Bonniebrook, Rose began receiving charming unsigned letters. By and by one of the letters was signed Harry Leon Wilson. The letters continued for months. Then Rose and her sister Callista returned to New York and her courtship by Harry began in earnest. In 1902, Rose and Harry were married in Jersey City, New Jersey, but there were difficulties in their rapport. Harry's moods reduced Rose to absolute silence. Again, Rose retreated to Bonniebrook. When she expressed no desire to return to New York, her mother suggested she didn't need to go back. Rose and Harry were divorced in 1908.

In 1909, Rose created the Kewpie doll, a roly-poly elf with a fat child's body, small wings, and a turnip-top head. These cupids had appeared in head and tail pieces when Rose illustrated love stories in books and magazines. Edward Bok of the *Ladies Home Journal* cut out a number of these and sent them to Rose, asking if she could make a series of illustrations of the little creatures. He told her he would find someone to make accompanying verses, but Rose wasn't about to allow anyone else to supply the dialogue for the series. Thus the Kewpie, a benevolent elf who did good deeds in a funny way, was created by Rose herself. "Kewpie" was an original name coined by Rose for her little cupid-like creations with tiny wings. She thought spelling it with a "K" seemed funnier.

Using the Kewpies, Rose illustrated her children's poems in *Woman's Home Companion* and *Good Housekeeping* magazines, as well as in books, Sunday cartoons, and cutouts (paper dolls). These stories were a two-page format of illustrations and rhymes. In 1909, Kewpies became a series in the *Ladies Home Journal*. In 1910, *Woman's Home Companion,* and later *Good Housekeeping,* carried the Kewpieville series. Also in 1910, *The Kewpies and Dottie Darling,*

a children's book written and illustrated by Rose, was published.

Children began yearning for a Kewpie doll they could hold. Rose was in Paris, where she was attending art school, making two pages of Kewpie adventures every month, illustrating stories for other magazines, as well as drawing "monsters" for her own personal satisfaction. She had not forgotten she was to model a Kewpie to be molded into a doll. She had made a beginning but as she had propped the figure only with a paintbrush, it had fallen over under the impact of her little Breton maid. As Rose was disinclined to start the formless mass again, she asked a young sculpture student to help. Rose had already made some well rounded-out drawings of a standing Kewpie, showing the proper size and three views: front, side, and back. The student came and "set up" the statue, but by the end of the day it looked as if there would be nothing Kewpish from the student's efforts. She had set up a solid first statue of a human child. Since the student was unable to sculpt a Kewpie to Rose's standards, Rose had to take matters into her own hands and her own darling Kewpie—with the absurd dimensions, tummy, topknot, wings, smile and all—was developed. George F. Borgfeldt & Company, the leading importer of toys at that time, asked that the statuette be delivered to their Paris office. From there, the Kewpie was sent off to the toy factories in Germany, taking his smile along with him.

The first fruits of the factories were a shocking travesty of the Kewpie's face and form. For some unknown reason, the factory had not cast the mold from the statuette. Some trusty "hand" had made a copy . . . well baked and all achieved in beautiful bisque. Rose went directly to Berlin. She stayed among the ancestral doll factories in the Thuringer Wald area of Germany until she had modeled twelve sizes of Kewpies and

launched the factories. Prior to World War I, Kewpies were made of bisque in German factories. Due to the shipping embargo during the war, they were later made of bisque, wood pulp or composition, chalk, and celluloid in the United States.

1911 saw publication of *The Kewpies Their Book*, a children's book by Rose. In 1913, Rose obtained the first patent in the United States for a three dimensional Kewpie Doll. The *Kewpie Kutouts* book by Rose was published in 1914, and *The Kewpie Primer*, a reading book for children illustrated by Rose, was published in 1916. During the 1920s, Kewpies appeared in *Good Housekeeping*, *The Delineator*, and *Ladies Home Journal*.

Rose's next doll, Scootles, the Baby Tourist who visited Kewpieville in her Kewpie stories, was created in 1923. This doll was sculpted as a real baby.

Rose with unidentified child and Cuddle Kewpies.

Rose's advertising campaigns included Edison Phonographs, Pratt & Lambert Paints and Varnishes, Kellogg's Corn Flakes, Rock Island Railroad, and Oxydol Detergent. Her series of ninety-eight Jell-O gelatin ads spanned the years 1909 to 1922 and included a series of Jell-O premium cookbooks. These are displayed at the Jell-O museum in Leroy, New York.

In 1921, Rose held a one-woman exhibit of her serious artwork, which she called "Sweet Monsters," at the Gallerie Devambez in Paris. These drawings are at the same time mysterious and revealing, exalted and terrifying. They show another facet of this amazing artist's depth of creativity. In 1922, the Sweet Monsters were exhibited at the Wildenstein and Company exhibition showrooms in New York City.

During the period from 1904 to 1930, Rose published several books while illustrating scores of other authors' works. Her first novel, *The Loves of Edwy*, was published in 1904 and *The Lady in the White Veil*, with five illustrations, followed in 1909. Rose's poetry book, *Master Mistress*, was published in 1922, and her story book, *The Kewpies and the Runaway Baby*, was published in 1928. Two more novels followed soon after: *Garda* in 1929 and *The Goblin Woman* in 1930.

In 1936, Rose and Callista returned to Bonniebrook to care for their ailing mother. Rose found herself destitute—her artwork was passé. She made a series of pin-ups drawings of Vargas-type girls but was never able to regain her former glory.

In 1940, Rose sculpted a squatty little laughing Buddha she called Ho-Ho. These were made using a rubber mold and plaster of Paris in three sizes. Unfortunately, Japan bombed Pearl Harbor on December 7, 1941 and the Buddha-like figurine never became popular.

Rose passed away on April 6, 1944 in Springfield, Missouri, after suffering a series of mild strokes. She is buried in the family cemetery at her beloved Bonniebrook.

In April 1967, a group of Rose O'Neill admirers met in Branson, Missouri. They formed what was later to be called the International Rose O'Neill Club (IROC). Three to five hundred loyal Rose O'Neill memorabilia collectors from all over the world meet in Branson each year to enjoy fellowship, swap treasures, and learn more about the life and artistic feats of this remarkable woman. To learn more about this club, please visit their Internet site at http://www.kewpierroseoneillclub.com or write to International Rose O'Neill Club, PO Box 668, Branson, Missouri, 65616.

The Bonniebrook Historical Society (BHS) was founded in 1975 to raise money to replicate Rose O'Neill's home at Bonniebrook. (The original house burned to the ground in 1947.) Through donations, the house was completed in 1993. The Society has since

Rose with kittens at her home, Carabus, in Westport, Connecticut.

added the Rose O'Neill Kewpie Museum and Gallery, a gift shop, and banquet room in the Maggie Fisher Centre. More information is available at their Internet site, http://www.kewpie-museum.com, or by writing to Bonniebrook Historical Society, PO Box 263, Branson, Missouri, 65615.

Rose has twice been recognized by the United States Postal Service with stamps commemorating her work. In 1997, Scootles appeared in the collection of *Classic American Dolls* and in 2000, Kewpie and Kewpidoodle were featured with nineteen other outstanding *American Illustrators*.

To learn more about the life of Rose O'Neill, we recommend three books. *The One Rose*, written by Rowena Godding Ruggles in 1964, is in its second edition but will probably have to be purchased on the secondary market. *Titans and Kewpies, The Life and Art of Rose O'Neill* was written by Ralph Alan McCanse and published in 1968 by Vantage Press, Inc., New York, New York. *The Story of Rose O'Neill*, an autobiography edited by Miriam Formanek-Brunell, was published in 1997 by the University of Missouri Press, Columbia, Missouri, 65201.

Chapter One

Bisque Kewpies

In 1913, Rose O'Neill obtained the first patent for the three dimensional Kewpie Doll. The Kewpie craze was at its peak in 1914 when the war in Europe broke out. Because of the war, shipments were cut off. One of Rose's saddest moments was when she heard that a ship full of Kewpies bound for America had sunk in the English Channel. By 1916, German toys had practically disappeared from store shelves and by 1917 they were entirely gone. So the German bisque Kewpies were only available for a very short period of time.

The term action Kewpie refers to any Kewpie that varies from the straight-legged, jointed-arm Kewpie. This includes Kewpies with an item added, such as a vase, basket, animal, hat, gun, sword, or flower. Bisque action Kewpies came in various sizes. Some sizes of the same action Kewpie are rarer than others. When determining the correct price for your particular Kewpie, you will need to ascertain its size.

Some Kewpies are identifiable by name. The Huggers, which are two Kewpies embracing, are the most common action Kewpies. They were very popular wedding decorations. The Kewpie Traveler is recognizable by his suitcase and umbrella. Blunderboo is the clumsy Kewpie. He is usually found in a fallen, awkward position. The Thinker is the seated Kewpie with elbows on knees and chin resting on hands. The Governor is seated in a chair with arms crossed over his chest. Mary Jane Kewpie has shoes and socks painted on before firing. Kewpie Gardener has a bisque, wide-brimmed straw-like hat and holds a rake. There is also an action Kewpie without the hat holding his arm out. This Kewpie can be found holding either a flower or flag. The Bellhop wears a pillbox hat and molded short jacket. Some of the rarer Kewpies are the "O" mouthed or opened mouth Kewpies. They have a surprised look on their faces or a wide Kewpie smile. The Hottentot is the name given by Rose to the black Kewpie.

Author Booth Tarkington gave Harry Wilson, Rose's second husband, a French bulldog puppy. He was white with a rakish patch over one eye, plump contours, a babyish round forehead, and a wide smile. He sat in a highchair beside Harry at the table, and accompanied him on his walks. Rose made portraits of him in his youth and some years later drew him as the Kewpies' dog, giving him little wings so he could fly with them. The Kewpies named him Kewpidoodle. When the Kewpie dolls arrived, he also was made as a little statue in bisque.

Artisans today are molding porcelain Kewpies. Some of these are hard to discern from the old German original Kewpies. However, if you put a reproduction next to an original German bisque Kewpie, the superior quality of expression and materials on the original becomes readily apparent.

3" Kewpie and girl with 2" Kewpie on table, 4.25" x 3.5" base, ©, 549 and crown on bottom, $6000-7000.

12" x 11.5" Kewpie Mound consists of twenty-three bisque action Kewpies and one Kewpidoodle Dog placed on a bisque mound, $50,000-75,000.

4" Kewpie sitting at all bisque table and chair with three piece tea set and plate of breakfast food, $3200-3500.

3.5" Kewpie with 3.25" elephant, shield paper label, 9378 incised on backside of elephant, $6000-8000.

Back view of Kewpie with the elephant.

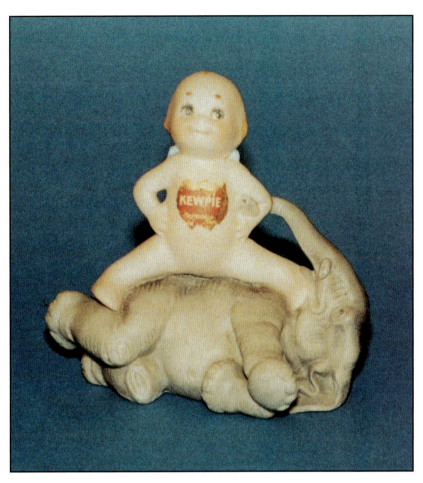

2.75" Kewpie doing splits atop a 4" x 4" elephant, incised 9381, paper shield, © paper circle on back, $6000-8000.

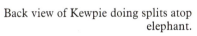

Back view of Kewpie doing splits atop elephant.

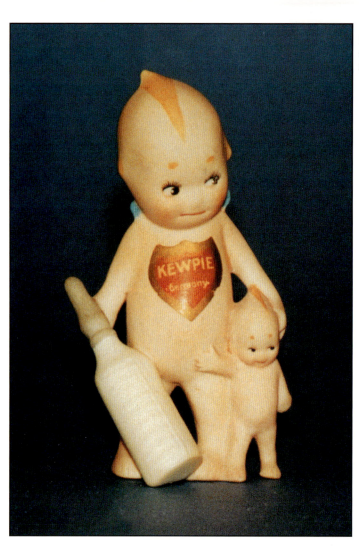

3.5" Kewpie with 1.5" Kewpie baby with bottle,
shield paper label, 87 incised on back of left leg,
$4700-5200.

4.25" Kewpie holding his 1.75" Teddy at side,
unmarked, $2000-2500.

4" Kewpie with a 1.75" dog standing
by its leg, no markings, $2000-2500.

2" bisque Kewpie standing with arms up, on the steps of a 2" x 1.5" beach bath house changing cart, © on bottom, incised 6738, $3500-4000.

Kewpie on an all bisque, wood-like cart trinket box, 3" x 2.75" x 2.5", Trademark, impressed crown with a WC under it, $3200-3500.

View of trinket box with lid removed.

1.75" Kewpie on 3.5" x 1.5" x 2.25" ink well, $650-850; 1.5" Blunderboo atop 2" x 2.5" sled, heart sticker, $600-800; Kewpie in bed trinket box, 2.5" x 1" x 2.5", no markings, $1000-1200.

1.5" Kewpidoodle Dog with 2" Kewpie sitting on 2.75" x 3.5" x 1.25" couch, $3500-4000; 2" mandolin playing Kewpie sitting in 3" x 2.25" x 2" chair, unusual because of bisque blanket, $3500-4000; 2" mandolin playing Kewpie sitting in 3" x 2.25" x 2" chair, unusual because of bisque blanket, $1200-1500.

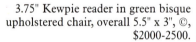

3.75" Kewpie reader in green bisque upholstered chair, overall 5.5" x 3", ©, $2000-2500.

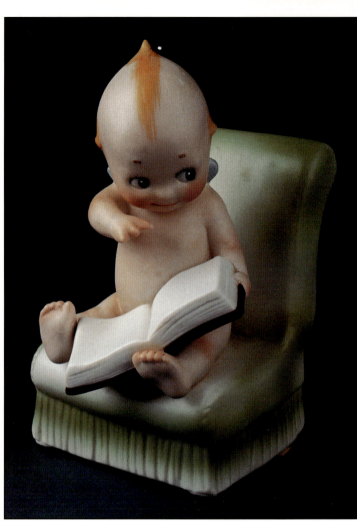

3.5" bisque Kewpie Governor with arms crossed in bisque wicker chair, © stamped on bottom, $500-600.

3.25" bisque Kewpie Governor with arms crossed and right foot over the left, sitting in a hooded wicker chair with "Boston" incised on the base, © stamped on the bottom, $600-800.

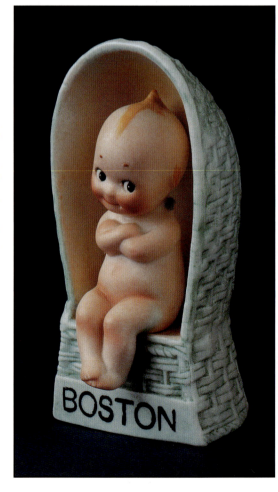

14

3.25" seated Kewpie in a 4.5" fan chair,
World's Fair 1915 souvenir, ©, $600-800.

3.25" bisque Kewpie Governor with arms
crossed and right foot over the left, sitting in a
hooded chair with "California" incised on the
base, gift shop item, ©, $600-800.

2.5" bisque Governor sitting with arms folded in a wicker armchair, shield
sticker, $400-500; 3" Kewpie holding a rose in his lap, sitting in a hooded
chair, © stamped, $500-700.

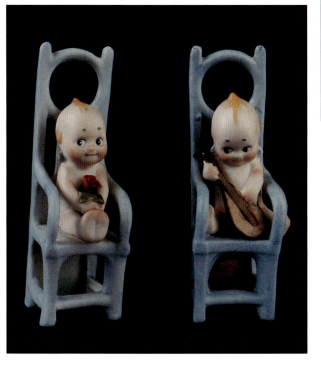

1.75" Kewpie sitting in 4" high back chair holding a rose in lap, $700-
900; 1.75" Kewpie holding a mandolin in 4" high back chair, ©
stamped on bottom, shield on bottom of chair, $700-900.

Kewpie coming out of egg, 3.5" x 5.75", heart sticker Kewpie Germany, crown on bottom, 978?-9780, $4000-5000.

Back view of Kewpie coming out of egg.

5.25" Kewpie Gardener beside broken egg vase, $3000-3200.

2" reader Kewpie sitting with egg, 2.5" x 3.25", © on bottom, $1200-1500.

3.5" salt and pepper shakers, boxer Kewpies standing by broken egg jar, des. pat. sticker, Kewpies incised 4484, egg incised 4484C, $4000-4500.

A bisque, rabbit-drawn broken egg on wheels with a 2.25" Kewpie riding on the rabbit's back, ©, 3.5" x 2" base, $4500-5000.

3.5" bisque seated Kewpie on a 5.5" x 3.5" base with an open pot decorated with garlands of greenery and roses with a chicken, © on the bottom, Goebel, $3000-3200.

Flower basket with Kewpie peeking over the side, 2.5" x 3.5" x 1.5", marked 9820 with crown, $1500-1900.

4" seated Kewpie with wicker basket, marked 4874, ©, $1200-1400; 4" Kewpie on knees in front of wicker basket, $1200-1400.

4" Kewpie seated beside basket with arms out, garland on head added by owner, ©, Kewpie incised O'Neill, basket incised 9A, 92, $1200-1400.

3.5" seated bisque Kewpie leaning against a woven basket, "W" for Walterhausen, Germany, is incised on the basket, © on bottom, $1000-1200; 4.5" Careful of His Voice with scarf standing in front of a brown box, $1200-1400; 4.5" bisque Kewpie standing on base, pulling the drawstring at the top of a bag, marked O'Neill, 5520, Goebel, $1000-1200.

2" mandolin playing Kewpie seated in front of 2.25" x 1.25" green basket, $800-1000.

4.5" sitting Kewpie attached to wash basket, right arm forward with ladybug, ©, $1800-2000.

3.75" Spanish Kewpie with mantilla and fan, cup marked LS, 7, 14 on side, crown with W/C on bottom, $2500-2800.

2" x 1" blue basket weave trinket box, 2.5" kicking Kewpie laying on lid, ©, $1000-1200.

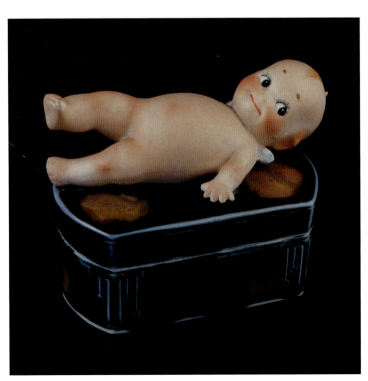

4.5" kicking Kewpie on 4" x 2.25" trinket box, incised with crown, W/C, 95, DePose, $1000-1200.

1.5" x 4" x 2.25" trinket box with 4.5" kicking Kewpie, ©, crown W/ C, DePose, 95, 8X, $800-1000.

3.5" round trinket dish with 1.75" sitting Kewpie holding rose on lap on the lid, $1000-1200.

5.25" bisque Aviator with helmet, goggles, and binoculars standing on base by a white flower vase with raised Kewpie swinging on a garland, Goebel mark on bottom, $3500-4000.

4.5" covered heart-shaped, three-color trinket dish with bisque Kewpie kicking his leg, Goebel, $1200-1500.

5.5" Kewpie Gardener holding rake, standing on a base with 6.5" floral decorated vase with purple shading, © stamped on bottom, Goebel, $1000-1500; 5.5" French Soldier with rifle and sword, standing on base with 6.5" bisque lavender shaded vase, $1000-1500.

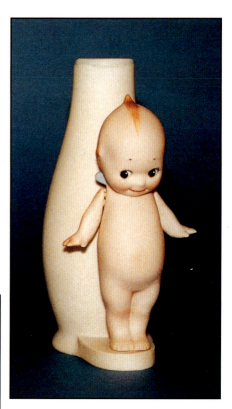

5" Kewpie with moveable arms on 6.25" bud vase, ©, incised crown W/C DePose, $3000-3500.

7" bisque candle holder with 5.25" Kewpie, jointed arms on base in the front, heart sticker and © on bottom, incised crown DePose, W/C mark Goebel, $3500-4000.

7" bisque candle holder with Kewpie Gardener holding his rake, Goebel, $3000-3500.

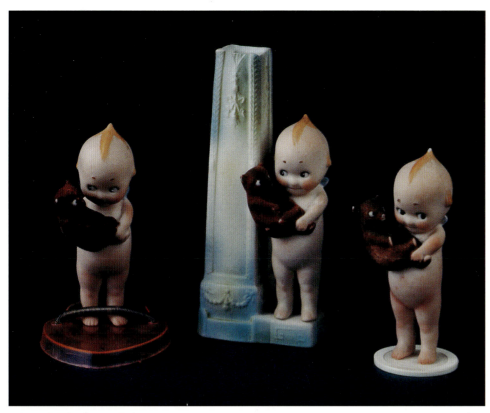

3.5" bisque Kewpie holding flocked brown bear, © on bottom, $600-800; 3.5" Kewpie holding flocked brown bear, standing on a base left of a 5.25" blue and ivory vase with squared corners, $800-1000; 3.5" Kewpie holding a bear standing on a base marked Goebel, $700-900.

5.5" Sweeper Kewpie on 2.75" x 2.75" planter with two fluted columns, Rose O'Neill circle copyright sticker, ©, 51, incised 4888 on base, $1400-1600.

3.5" standing Kewpie playing drum, no sticker, $2500-3000; 3.75" guitar playing Kewpie, standing on a base left of a 5.25" blue and ivory vase with squared corners, $800-1000; 3.5" guitar playing Kewpie beside an egg-shaped vase, marked 4854/c, 12, on vase, 4854 on foot of Kewpie, $1200-1500; 3.5" Kewpie guitar player, $600-800.

3.5" seated Kewpie, arms back, heart-shape dish, © stamped on bottom, $1200-1400.

3.5" seated Kewpie in 4.75" x 4.25" ash tray, heart sticker, ©, $1200-1400.

Soldier on pin tray, 1.75" x 4.25" x 2.5", pin tray marked 4897, O'Neill underneath rim, © and 43 on bottom, replacement fly, $1200-1400.

5.5" Kewpie Gardener with butterfly net standing in a gold cup on handle of a 10" x 7" green with pink and lavender flowered footed basket, incised 7880, Goebel, $4000-4500.

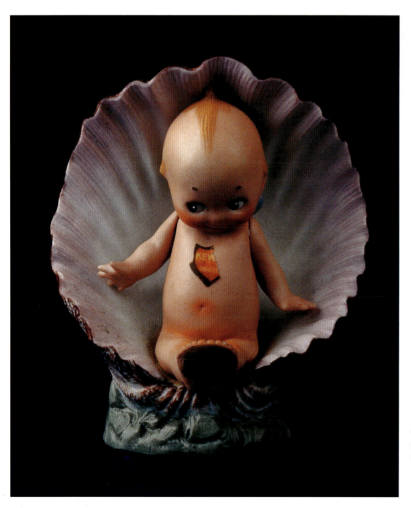

4" bisque jointed arms Kewpie sitting in a 6" x 5" shell on a green base, shield sticker on chest, © Rose O'Neill sticker on bottom, Goebel, $4000-4500.

2" Kewpie reader place card holder, $800-1000; 1.75" Kewpie with yellow rose place card holder, slot for card is in top of rose, $1000-1200; 2" Kewpie reader beside a blue wicker basket with lid leaning against the back, ©, $1000-1200; 2" Kewpie with heart atop Valentine card, $600-800.

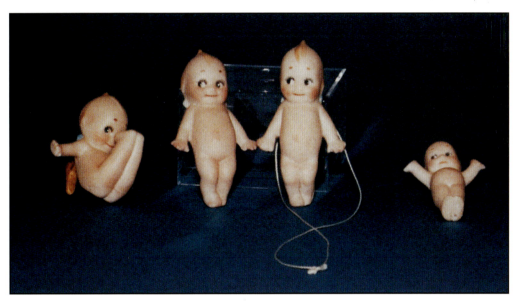

3" Kewpie with white jar between his legs, shield sticker, des. pat., Germany, $800-1000.

Tiny bisque Kewpies: 1.75" Blunderboo cup hook/place card holder, ©, 9065, $400-600; 2.75" Kewpie with bent knees place card holder/cup hook, $300-500; 2.5" Kewpie with loop on back, circle patent sticker, $300-500; 2" Kewpie with wide ribbon loop, circle patent sticker, $400-600.

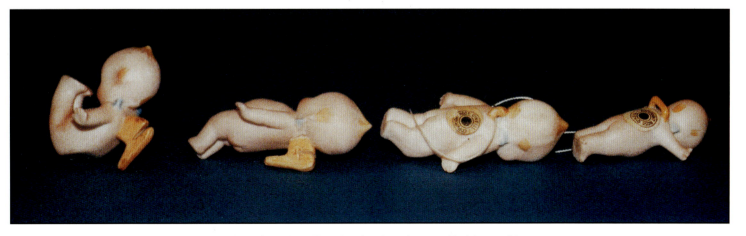

Back view of previous Kewpies showing place card holders and loops.

Four bisque bud vase/place card holders: 2.5" Kewpie with pen, shield on vase, © sticker on back, stamped © on bottom, $600-800; 2.5" Kewpie reading book, ©, $500-600; 2.5" Kewpie playing mandolin, © on bottom of vase, $500-600; 2.5" sitting Kewpie holding a rose in lap, © on bottom of vase, $500-600.

2.5" place card, bisque standing Kewpie with champagne bottle, paper sticker, and © stamped on back, $800-1000.

2.25" kicking Kewpie place card, incised 94, © Rose O'Neill sticker, $400-600; 1.25" Blunderboo Kewpie on 2.75" x 1.25" place card, heart sticker, © Rose O'Neill sticker, hole on place card behind Kewpie with string for hanging, $600-800; 2" Kewpie reader place card, ©, $300-500; 2" mandolin playing Kewpie on place card, incised 5514, $300-500.

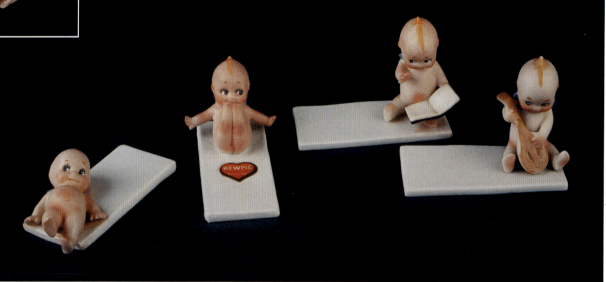

Two 2" seated mandolin players, $200-300 each; 2" mandolin player on pin tray, $800-1000; 2" mandolin player Kewpie bottle stopper, missing cork, $600-800.

3.75" Kewpie reader, ©, incised O'Neill, 97, $600-800; 2" Kewpie with pen on place card, ©, $400-600; 3" Kewpie with pen on 1.75" x 2" x 3.75" china ink well, ©, $1000-1200; 2" Kewpie with pen on 1.5" x 1.75" x 2.25" china ink well, heart sticker, ©, incised O'Neill, $800-1000; 3.5" Kewpie with pen, $600-800; 3.5" Kewpie with pen on porcelain 3" x 5" postcard, reads, "With Kewpish love from Rose O'Neill," cancelled stamp, $1000-1200.

2.5" Kewpie with Kewpidoodle Dog, heart sticker, round © sticker on back, 1913, incised made in Japan, $200-400; 2.5" seated Kewpie in wicker chair, heart sticker, made in Japan, $150-300; back view of previous chair; 3" seated Kewpie with black top hat, shield sticker, Germany, $400-600.

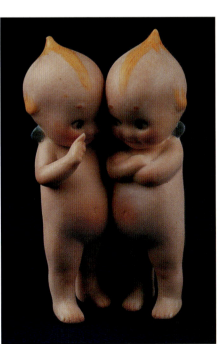

3.5" instructor Kewpie with stubborn friend, ©, $1200-1500.

3.75" bisque Hugger Kewpies dressed in replica patriotic outfits of the Belgian and American flags, $400-600.

3.75" bisque Hugger Kewpies in original crepe paper nurse and soldier outfits, $400-600.

3.5" Kewpie Huggers, made in Germany, $200-400; 3.5" Kewpie huggers, heart sticker, made in Japan, $150-250.

3.5" Kewpie readers or lawyers with brown book against legs, $600-800.

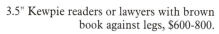

4" Kewpie bride and groom, made in Japan, $125-150.

4.5" reproduction seated Kewpie in blue chair, made in Japan, $50-100; 7" standing Kewpie, heart sticker, made in Japan, $150-250.

4.5" blue glazed porcelain perfume bottle, heart sticker with Kewpie Germany, © on back, $1000-1200; 3.5" bisque Kewpie with cork in back, unmarked, $800-1000.

4.5" bisque perfume bottle, heart sticker, $1000-1200; 3.5" bisque Kewpie perfume bottle with cork in back, $800-1000.

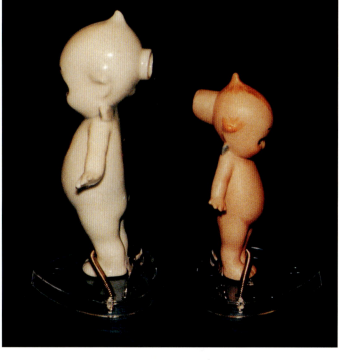

Side view of above Kewpies.

3.5" perfume holder, 2" Kewpie seated with chick hatching from egg, marked 5014, Germany, metal stopper on side of head, $1800-2000.

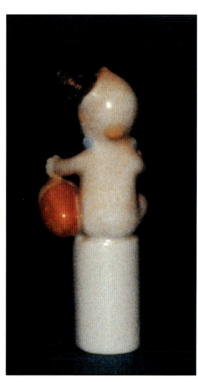

Back view of 2" Kewpie perfume holder.

3" cork bottle stopper with 2" Kewpie holding mandolin, $800-1000.

2" seated Kewpie with arms outstretched stopper atop a 7" blue perfume bottle, $800-1000.

4.5" bisque action Kewpie, with arm extended to hold object, $600-800.

4.5" Kewpie with extended arm, ribbon skirt and crepe paper basket are as found, O'Neill incised on feet, ©, $600-800.

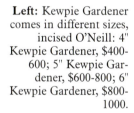

Left: Kewpie Gardener comes in different sizes, incised O'Neill: 4" Kewpie Gardener, $400-600; 5" Kewpie Gardener, $600-800; 6" Kewpie Gardener, $800-1000.

Right: Kewpie carrying wheat and sickle, shield sticker, $2000-2500.

4.5" Kewpie in red and white stripe painted-on swimsuit carrying a sand pail; 4.5" Kewpie in blue and white stripe suit carrying a shovel, $1800-2200 each.

5.5" Rough Rider Kewpie, shield sticker, copyright circle sticker on back, O'Neill incised on feet, $2000-2400; 5.25" Farmer with blue overalls, shield sticker, O'Neill incised on feet, $2000-2400.

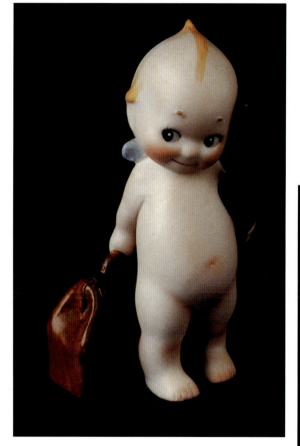

3.5" Kewpie Sweeper, incised O'Neill, ©, $600-800; 4.75" Kewpie sweeper, ©, incised O'Neill, $800-1000.

Kewpie Traveler with valise and umbrella is found in different sizes, incised 4916 and O'Neill, ©: 2.5" Kewpie, $200-300; 3.5" Kewpie, $300-400; 4.5" Kewpie, $400-500; 5" Kewpie, $500-600.

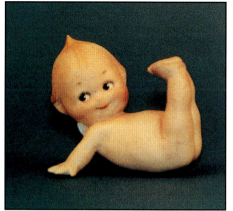

Blunderboo on back, 2.5" x 2.75", $1000-1200.

3.25" seated Kewpie with arms forward and hole for bug, ©, incised O'Neill, $400-600; 3.25" seated Kewpie with arms back, ©, incised 62, $400-600.

4.5" seated Kewpie with bug on foot, arms forward, red shield sticker, ©, incised O'Neill, $1000-1200; 3.25" seated Kewpie with arms back, ladybug on foot, red shield sticker, $600-800.

2.5" Kewpie cup hook/place card holder with bent knees, $300-500; 1.5" Blunderboo Kewpie on 2" x 1" sled, ©, $600-800; 1.5" Blunderboo Kewpie place card holder, incised O'Neill, 4906A, $400-600.

4.25" seated and reaching out with right arm, ©, ladybug missing from forehead, unreadable number, incised O'Neill, $700-900; 3.75" kneeling Kewpie, red heart sticker, incised O'Neill, ©, $800-1000; 4" seated with right arm out, incised O'Neill, 8, $600-800.

4.5" seated Kewpie with hands by head and feet together, shield sticker, incised O'Neill on bottom, $800-1000.

3.5" seated Kewpie with black cat on his lap, $500-700; 3.25" seated Kewpie with gray flocked cat, $500-700.

3.25" seated Kewpies with cats on laps, ©, black flocked cats incised 95, tan flocked cat and white bisque cat, $500-700 each.

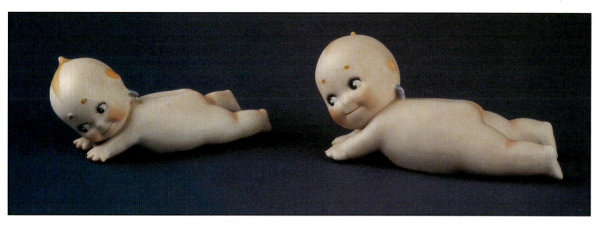

4" Kewpie laying on stomach, incised O'Neill, 5517, ©, sticker, $400-600; 3.5" Kewpie laying on stomach, incised O'Neill, A, 4862, 92, ©, $500-700.

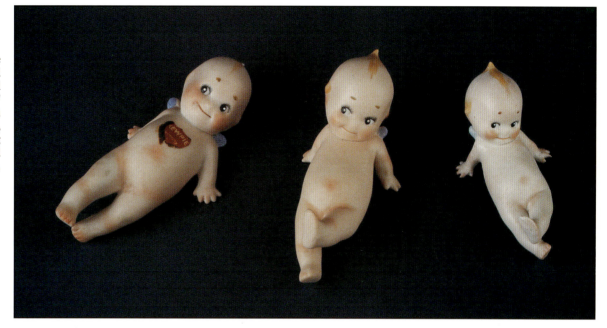

4.75" kicking Kewpie indented on bottom, red shield sticker, incised 5519, $600-800; 4.25" kicking Kewpie with head up, incised 5518, $600-800; 3.5" kicking Kewpie, ©, incised O'Neill, 4877, $600-800.

2.5" buttonhole Kewpie with moveable arms, $300-400; 2.5" buttonhole Kewpie, moveable arms, $300-400; 2" buttonhole Kewpie with arms up, $200-300; 2.5" Kewpie holding arms in front, $300-400.

2.75" Kewpie holding Valentine card with red heart on top, $600-800.

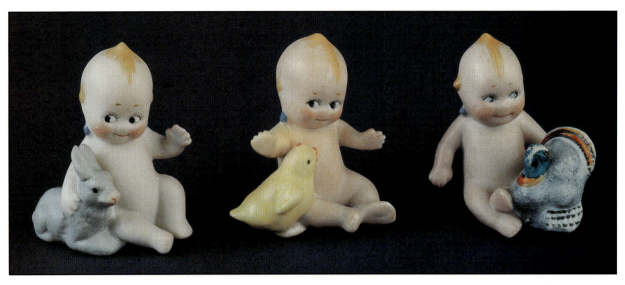

2" Kewpie with gray rabbit at right side, $500-700; 2" Kewpie with chick at right side, $500-700; 2" Kcwpic with turkey at left side, circle patent sticker, 1913, Germany, $500-700.

2" seated Kewpie holding flower with flower pot at his back and rose which is open to hold place card, $500-700; 2" seated Kewpie holding a pair of gold rings , $500-700; 2" Kewpie holding pumpkin in front, circle patent sticker, 1913, Germany, $500-700; 2" Kewpie with shamrock and crock of gold, $400-600.

3.5" Kewpie with goose, stick pin holder, marked 4488 on bottom of goose, $1800-2000.

Back view of Kewpie with goose.

4.5" Kewpie Bellhop, blue uniform with red cap, incised O'Neill, $1400-1600; 3.75" German cadet or bellhop dressed in green, ©, $800-1000.

4.5" Kewpie Bellhop, blue uniform with red cap, $1200-1400.

5.5" Kewpie Bellhop with molded hat and chin strap, jointed arms, incised O'Neill, $1400-1600.

4.5" Kewpie Firemen, shield stickers, copyright circle stickers on back, one with red hat with black helmet numbered 206, the other with a black hat with red helmet numbered 206, $1800-2000 each.

4.25" Kewpie Policeman, jointed arms, red shield, $1200-1500; 4.25" Kewpie Policeman with molded arms, ©, $1200-1500.

3.25" flag waving action Kewpie, Kewpie Germany shield sticker, incised O'Neill on bottom, $1600-1800.

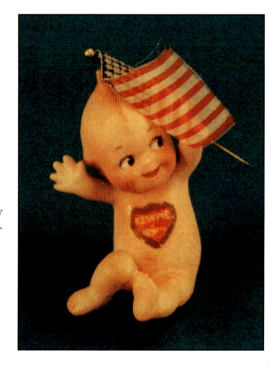

3.75" running Kewpie holding a flag, shield sticker, $1000-1200.

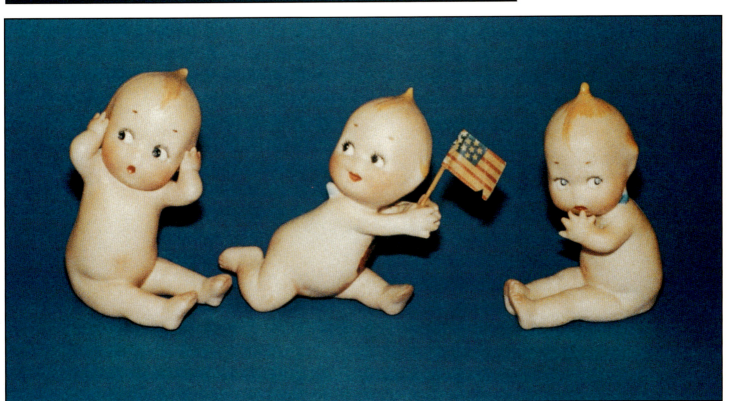

3.25" "O" mouth seated Kewpie with hands to ears, incised O'Neill #15, copyright sticker on back, $800-1000;
3.25" Kewpie with open smile mouth, shield sticker, copyright circle on back, $800-1000; 3.25" seated "O"
mouth Kewpie with hand to mouth, incised O'Neill on feet, #23, copyright circle on back, $800-1000.

4.25" "O" mouth crawling Kewpie, circle © sticker, incised O'Neill, $1000-1200; 3.25" "O" mouth Kewpie with hand to mouth, incised O'Neill, $800-1000; 3.25" "O" mouth Kewpie with hands to ears, incised O'Neill, $800-1000.

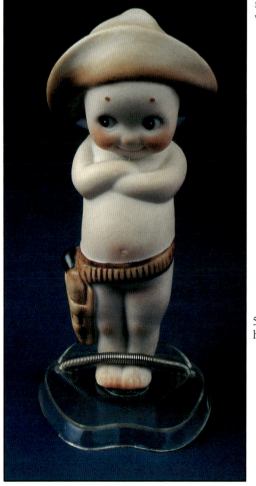

5" Cowboy Kewpie wearing hat, gun, and holster, patent sticker, $2000-2400.

3.75" Kewpie Indian in molded clothes, O'Neill on feet, $1500-1800.

4.25" Kewpie Pirate or Sailor, molded clothes, incised O'Neill, had a shield sticker on top of hat, $1500-1800.

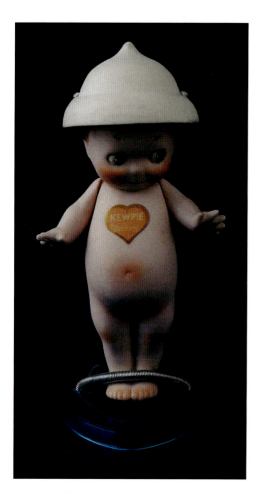

5.5" swivel-headed Kewpie, this side features smiling Kewpie, moveable hat held to head by cord attached through holes above the ears, heart sticker, incised O'Neill, $2000-2500.

2" Kewpie standing behind brown shoe, overall size 2.5", ©, 5568, $2000-2500.

Head turned on previous 5.5" swivel-headed Kewpie, showing "O" mouth with tears on cheeks.

Back view of swivel-headed Kewpie showing molded wings.

4.25" standing Kewpie with gray hat and umbrella, $1800-2000.

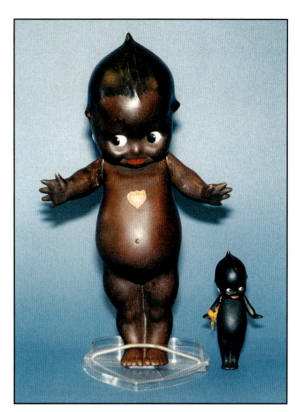

12" Hottentot Kewpie, marked O'Neill, paper shield on front "Glucks Kind," $2400-2600; 4.5" Hottentot, marked O'Neill on feet, $600-800.

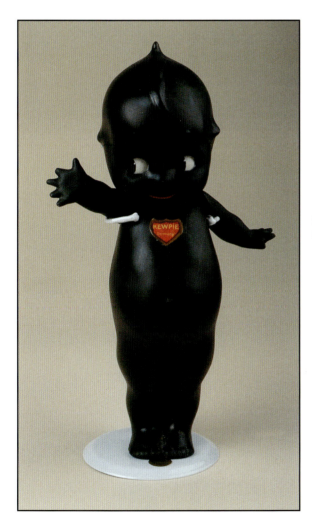

9" Black bisque Hottentot Kewpie with stickers, $1800-2000.

4.5" Hottentot Kewpie with watermelon mouth and brown hair, shield sticker, O'Neill incised on feet, $600-800; 5.25" Hottentot Kewpie with jointed arms, O'Neill incised on feet, $800-1000.

4.5" Hottentot Kewpie
with front shield and
back circle paper labels,
$600-800.

Back view of 4.5" Hottentot
Kewpie showing circle paper
label.

3.5" bisque Kewpie Traveler with umbrella and valise, dressed as
Santa in red crepe paper, accessories include metal skates and
frozen Charlotte doll, $1200-1500.

5" original dressed Kewpies, both
incised O'Neill on bottom of feet: one
wears Mary Jane slippers and Safety
First pin, $600-800; the other in
Halloween costume has original
witchery paint on face, $300-400.

4.25" straight-legged bride and groom Kewpies with jointed arms, $400-600.

5.25" Hawaiian grass skirted Kewpie with lei, tied to a red velvet base, $400-600.

5" Kewpie with Mary Jane shoes, jointed arms, heart sticker, $500-700; 4.5" dressed Kewpie with Mary Jane shoes, $400-600.

5.25" Scottish Kewpie in kilt, sash, and tam, $600-800; 5.25" dressed Kewpie, $300-400; 5.25" dressed Kewpie, $300-400; 5.25" Kewpie wearing a gray fox stole, $300-400.

5.25" Kewpie dressed as Little Red Riding Hood, wearing Mary Jane shoes, $700-900.

6" straight-legged Kewpie in satin fairy costume with wings and jointed arms, round German marking printed on back, $300-500.

4.5" Mardi Gras dressed Kewpie with mask, $300-400; 4.5" dressed Kewpie, $200-300; 4.5" dressed Kewpie, $200-300.

Four 4.5" dressed Kewpies, $200-300 each.

Four additional 4.5" dressed Kewpies, $200-300 each.

4.25" preacher, $200-300; 4.5" bride dressed Kewpie, lace and net with satin ribbons, bouquet, $200-300; 4.25" groom dressed Kewpie, top hat, painted tuxedo, $200-300.

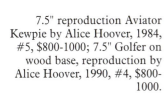

7.5" reproduction Aviator Kewpie by Alice Hoover, 1984, #5, $800-1000; 7.5" Golfer on wood base, reproduction by Alice Hoover, 1990, #4, $800-1000.

12.5" Kewpie doll, Alice Hoover reproduction, porcelain, glass-eyed, 1980, #24, $600-800.

12" glass goggly-eyed, bisque J.D.
Kestner Kewpie, original dotted
Swiss dress, composition jointed
body, incised on nape of neck, Ges.
Gesch O'Neill J.D.K., 11, $6500-7000;
13" original dress, same J.D.K.
markings, incised 12, $7000-7500; 13"
in cotton romper, same J.D.K.
markings, incised 12, $7000-7500.

13" J.D. Kestner glass goggly-eyed Kewpie, incised on neck
base, Ges. Gesch., O'Neill, J.D.K. 12, personally autographed
on foot by Rose O'Neill, $7500-8000.

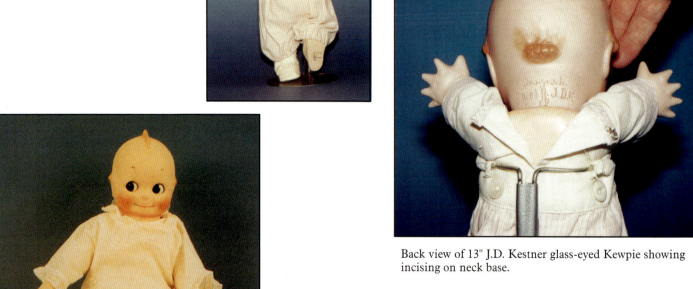

Back view of 13" J.D. Kestner glass-eyed Kewpie showing
incising on neck base.

11" bisque swivel head Kewpie on handmade cloth body, incised
on neck base, made in Germany, 1377, 2125, $2500-3000.

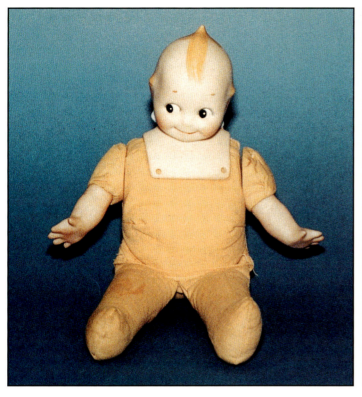

8" shoulder plate bisque head Kewpie with original cloth body and bisque half arms, incised on shoulder back 9268/4, $2200-2500.

Back view shows this Kewpie had a "cry-box."

3.25" Shoulder head Kewpie, 1.75" shoulders, marked 9268-4, made in Germany, $600-800; 2" flange-head Kewpie, marked 997/5/0, incised made in Germany, $500-700; 1.5" sew-on head, incised Germany, $400-600.

1.5" Kewpie half doll, arms up, pierced in four places, no markings, $300-500.

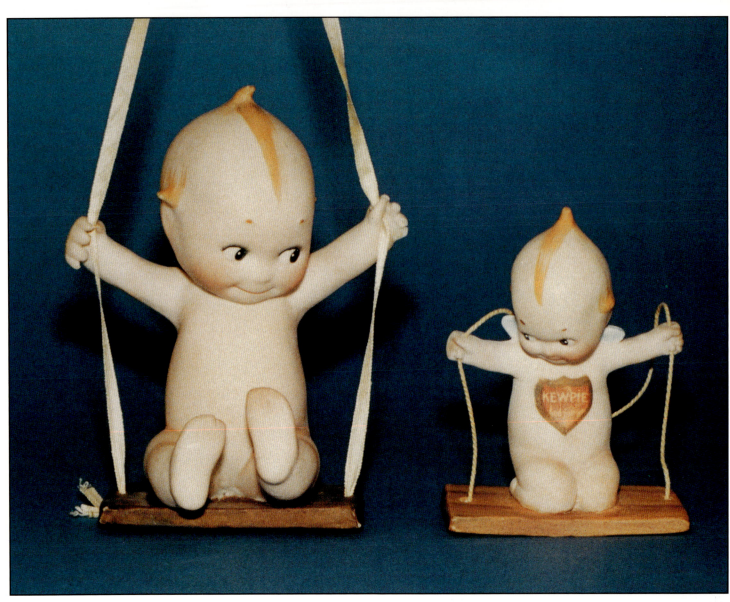

4.75" seated Kewpie on 3" x 1.75" swing, ©, $2400-2600; 3.25" kneeling Kewpie on 2.75" x 1.25" swing, shield sticker, ©, $2000-2200.

2.5" Kewpie on a 1.5" x 1.25" swing, © on bottom, $1800-2000.

2.5" bisque sitting Kewpie with rose in lap swinging in a hammock strung from a string, © stamped, $4000-4500.

2" Kewpie in swing over pin cushion, hands together holding rose, $400-600.

Bisque Thinkers seated with elbows on knees, chin resting on hands, incised O'Neill: 6.5" Kewpie Thinker, $600-800; 6" Kewpie Thinker, $500-700; 5.5" Kewpie Thinker, $400-600; 4.75" Kewpie Thinker, $350-500; 4.5" Kewpie Thinker, $300-400.

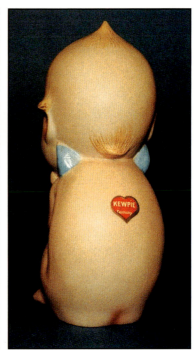

Left: 5" straight-legged Kewpie, $150-250; 7" Thinker Kewpie with heart sticker, Germany on the back, $800-1000; 4.25" Thinker Kewpie, $250-350.

Right: Back view of 7" Thinker with heart Kewpie German sticker, © round sticker and O'Neill signature incised on bottom.

6.25" plaster of Paris Kewpie Thinker, $400-600; 6.5" German bisque Kewpie Thinker, signed Rose O'Neill, Germany, across the lower back, $600-800.

Bottom view of previous Kewpie Thinker. Signed on the bottom by Rose O'Neill, "To my darling Maka, This little Kewpie smile from her. Rose O'Neill."

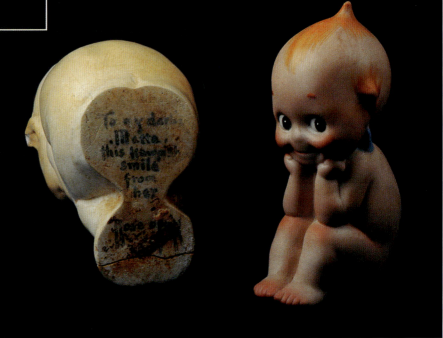

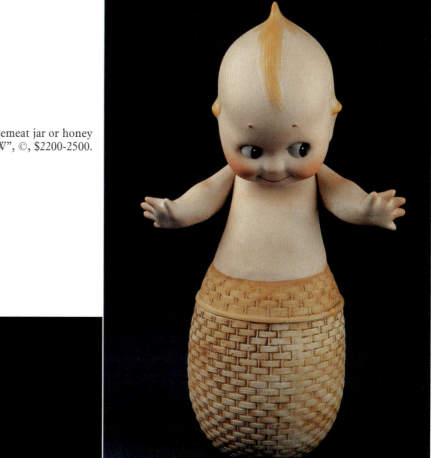

10.5" Kewpie woven mincemeat jar or honey pot, marked "W", ©, $2200-2500.

Separated Kewpie mincemeat jar or honey pot.

3.25" x 7.75" framed bisque plaque with six 2" Kewpies holding hands, $1200-1400.

4" Kewpie candy jar in green and white bisque dress, no markings, $600-800.

Separated Kewpie candy jar.

Back view of 7" x 2.5" bisque wall plaques.

7" x 2.5" bisque wall plaques, incised 5531, ©, on back. Copyright Rose O'Neill sticker on one, $1600-1800.

Seventeen bisque straight-legged Kewpies with moveable arms demonstrate the variety of sizes. It is possible Kewpies made from the same mold can vary fractions of an inch depending on the slip and firing techniques. Most of these Kewpies are original Rose O'Neill Kewpies made by J.D. Kestner.

This 9.25" straight bisque Kewpie pictured among the group above is an exception. It was made by Fulper in the U.S.A., $1000-1200.

Bisque straight-legged Kewpies: 9" Kewpie, $700-800; 13" with original box designed by Rose O'Neill, $1800-2000; 12" Kewpie, $1200-1500.

6.5" newer reproduction Kewpie and original box, red heart sticker, Rose O'Neill Kewpie Japan, $300-400.

7.5" original bisque Rose O'Neill Kewpies, incised on foot and with stickers, in box designed by Rose O'Neill, $600-800; 8.5" Kewpie, same as 7.5" Kewpie, $800-1000.

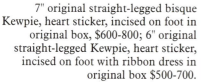

7" original straight-legged bisque Kewpie, heart sticker, incised on foot in original box, $600-800; 6" original straight-legged Kewpie, heart sticker, incised on foot with ribbon dress in original box $500-700.

5.5" original straight-legged bisque Kewpie in original box, stickers, $400-600; 5" original straight-legged Kewpie in original box, stickers, $300-500.

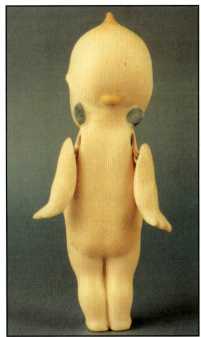

6.5" straight-legged Kewpie with jointed arms in original box, Germany incised on backside, $600-800

Back view of 6.5" straight-legged Kewpie showing Germany incised on backside.

6.5" bisque straight-legged Kewpie with jointed arms, personally autographed on feet by Rose O'Neill, $1000-1200.

Rose O'Neill autograph on feet of 6.5" Kewpie.

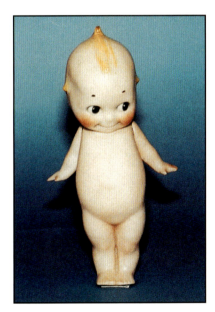

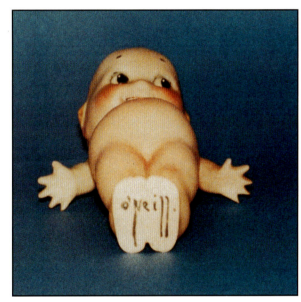

5.75" Nippon Kewpie with box, paper heart Kewpie Reg. US Pat Off, incised Nippon, paper label on feet, $400-600.

10.5" straight-legged bisque Kewpie with Mary Jane shoes and socks added before firing, by J. D. Kestner, stickers, very rare size, $1500-1800.

9" Kewpie, fully-jointed arms and hips, shield sticker, marked 4 arms, 185/4 legs, $1800-2000.

9.25" fully-jointed Kewpie, heart sticker, $2000-2200.

5" Kewpie, fully-jointed arms and hips, shield sticker, circle © sticker on back, $600-800.

Four sizes of fully-jointed arms and legs bisque Kewpies: 7.75" jointed Kewpie with red shield label, incised on legs and arms 2, $1200-1400; 6.25" Kewpie marked 185/0, $800-1000; 6" heart shaped label, incised 183/3/0, $700-900; 5" Kewpie with red shield label, arms marked 5/0, 185 on legs, $600-800.

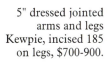

5" dressed jointed arms and legs Kewpie, incised 185 on legs, $700-900.

5.75" overall height of Kewpie on horse, 3.75" Kewpie wearing cavalry Prussian helmet with eagle on front, 4.5" long horse on 3.5" base, ©, 5597, crown with W/C, $6500-7500.

5.5" wounded bisque German Soldier, molded uniform in field gray, artillery helmet with ball top, brown boots, three cannon balls stacked at his feet, Kewpie Hero shield, incised O'Neill, $4500-5000; 4.5" dressed Kewpie Nurse with jointed arms, wearing Mary Jane shoes, incised O'Neill, separate metal Red Cross pin, $600-800.

5" German Soldier Kewpie with spiked helmet of battalion 31, molded rifle, sword on belt, $1200-1400.

4.5" molded German uniformed Kewpie with red piping around collar, sleeves, and front of jacket, molded rifle at side, ammunition belt with straps over the shoulders, and brown boots, Kewpie Hero shield on helmet, $2000-2400.

5.5" English Bobby or Soldier with molded clothes, jointed arms, belt holding a sword, paper shield on hat, Kewpie Germany, $1800-2000; 5.5" molded Soldier with helmet, 83 battalion number on helmet, rifle at arms and sword at side, ©, $1800-2000.

Front and back of 4.75" German Soldier, battalion 95 on helmet, sword up and scabbard on side, paper shield Kewpie Germany, patent circle, red 14 on bottom, $1200-1400.

4.75" German Cavalry Soldier known as Hassars with molded clothes and saddle, holding replaced flag, incised O'Neill 15, $5000-5500.

Molded infantry helmets with eagle and cross, rifle, and ammo case on waist: 5.75" Soldier, Kewpie Hero shield sticker, applied to stand, $2200-2600; 4.75" Infantry Soldier, marked 45, O'Neill on feet, $1800-2000.

Kewpie Infantry Soldiers: 5.75" with sash and sword, holding replaced flag, © O'Neill, $2000-2400; 5" with sash and sword, holding replaced flag, © O'Neill, $1800-2200; 3.75" Cavalry Soldier with saddle and sword, unmarked, $1600-1800.

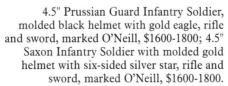

4.5" Prussian Guard Infantry Soldier, molded black helmet with gold eagle, rifle and sword, marked O'Neill, $1600-1800; 4.5" Saxon Infantry Soldier with molded gold helmet with six-sided silver star, rifle and sword, marked O'Neill, $1600-1800.

4.5" seated Prussian Soldier with jointed arms, incised 18 and 80, molded helmet with gold eagle, $2200-2400.

4.75" Prussian Infantry Kewpie Soldier in full headdress, pickelaube, molded rifle, sword on belt, Kewpie Hero shield, incised O'Neill, $1000-1500.

4.5" Prussian Infantry Soldier Kewpie with red bisque tassel on helmet, rifle damaged, sword on belt, without damage $1000-1500; 3.5" Prussian Infantry Soldier saluting, legs apart, sword at side, $1000-1200.

2.5" Prussian Rifle Battalion Kewpie with arms raised, bisque tassel, and field badge on helmet, $600-800; 2.5" Prussian Kewpie with arms raised, wearing the spiked top infantry helmet, $600-800.

5.5" Prussian Cavalry Soldier wearing a brown flocked busby with field badge and tassel, chin strap, molded red covered pouch on belt, hand on saber, saluting, $1600-1800.

4" German Soldiers with brown molded red flat top hats with gold garland and star on front, rifles and swords, incised O'Neill, one with red Kewpie Hero shield, $1000-1200 each.

3.5" German Soldier standing with legs apart, saluting, $1000-1200.

4" seated German Soldier, Kewpie Hero shield on front, $2200-2400.

6.25" Prussian Soldier with eagle atop helmet worn by the imperial bodyguards, Prussian Garde du Corps, sword over shoulder, scabbard at side, pouch on shoulder strap on back, ©, incised O'Neill, $3000-3400.

4.5" Belgium Infantryman wearing red banded field cap with badge, rifle and sword, paper shield Kewpie Germany, red 33 on bottom of feet, $1200-1400.

5.25" German Infantry Soldier with 32 embossed on helmet, holding rifle with sword at his side, painted shoes, $1200-1400; 5.25" dressed Kewpie, Mary Jane shoes, incised O'Neill on feet, $700-900.

4.75" German Infantryman wearing green badge field cap, Kewpie Germany shield, ©, rifle and sword, $1200-1400.

Two 4.5" French Kewpie Soldiers, holding rifles, molded swords in scabbard, $300-500 each; 3.75" French Soldier Kewpie, holding rifle, molded sword at side, shield sticker, $300-400.

4" French Kewpie Soldier wearing red kepi, rifle, sword in scabbard, heart sticker, patent sticker on back, $200-300; 4.5" French Kewpie Soldier on base with vase, rose garland decoration, ©, $2500-2800.

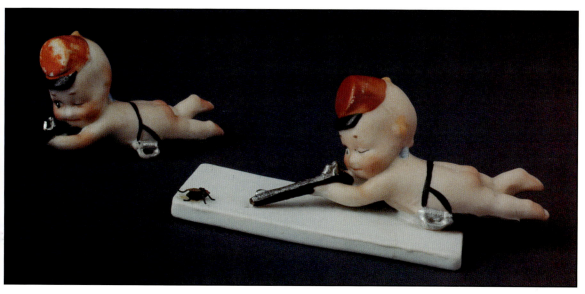

3" French Kewpie Soldier on stomach, aiming rifle with ammunition bag and saber at his side place card holder, ©, $1200-1500; 3" French Kewpie Soldier laying on place card aiming at fly, $800-1000.

4.25" Sailor Kewpie with molded dress white hat, jointed arms, incised O'Neill on feet, circle © sticker on back, $1200-1500.

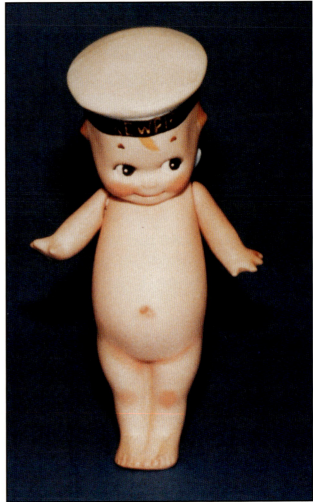

4.5" Sailor Kewpie with molded blue hat, jointed arms, heart sticker, $1200-1500.

3.5" seated Sailor, molded blue hat, "Kewpie" painted on band of hat, jointed arms, incised 18 and 87, $1800-2000.

Four original Rose O'Neill Kewpidoodle Dogs: 4" brown spotted Kewpidoodle Dog, incised Rose O'Neill 7, ©, $1800-2000; 3" black spotted Kewpidoodle Dog, incised Rose O'Neill 3, $1400-1600; 2.75" black spotted Kewpidoodle Dog, the dog was salvaged from the Bonniebrook fire, incised Rose O'Neill 3, $1400-1600; 1.5" brown spotted Kewpidoodle Dog, not incised, $1000-1200.

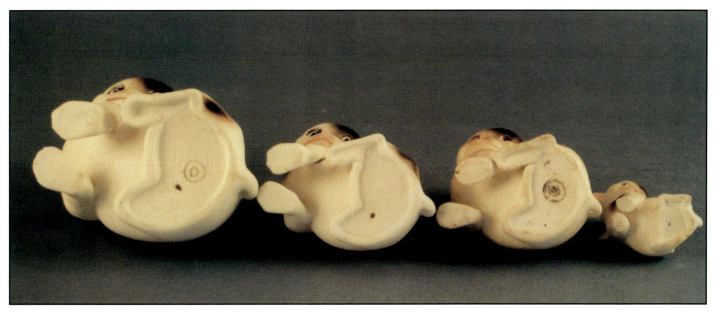

Bottom view of the four original Kewpidoodle Dogs. Note how closely the front and back paws are positioned. The back paw is indented like the bottom of the Kewpidoodle Dog.

Nine reproduction Kewpidoodle Dogs: 1.25" Kewpidoodle Dog by Connie Harrell, $25; 1.5" and 2" Kewpidoodle Dogs by Darlene Woods, $25 each; 2.25" Kewpidoodle Dog, incised Rose O'Neill 5, $25; 2.25" Carmen Jackson Kewpidoodle Dog, $25; four 2.25" Kewpidoodle Dogs, incised Rose O'Neill 5, $20.

Bottom view of the nine reproduction Kewpidoodle Dogs. Note that the bottom of the back paw on the reproduction has no indentation.

3" black spotted bisque Kewpidoodle Dog, ©, $1400-1600; 3" brown spotted Kewpidoodle Dog, ©, $1400-1600; 3.5" brown spotted Kewpidoodle Dog, ©, $1600-1800.

4.5" brown Kewpidoodle Dog, marked ©, incised Rose O'Neill 8, $2200-2400; 1.5" brown Kewpidoodle Dog, ©, $1000-1200.

2.5" Kewpidoodle Dog on a 2" base, incised 77, ©, $1200-1500.

3" Kewpidoodle Dog with wire fly, incised Rose O'Neill, 4, ©, $2000-2200.

3.5" Kewpie with 1.5" Kewpidoodle Dog, slit for mouth place card holder, bouquet in hand, © on foot, O'Neill on other foot, $2600-3000.

3.5" bisque Kewpie Traveler with bisque, black spotted Kewpidoodle Dog on leash, patent sticker, ©, $1500-1700; 3.5" bisque Kewpie Traveler with bisque, brown spotted Kewpidoodle Dog on leash, heart and patent sticker, ©, $1500-1700.

3.5" bisque Kewpie Traveler with black Kewpidoodle Dog on leash, circle patent sticker on back, ©, incised O'Neill, $1500-1700; 2.5" Kewpie Traveler with black Kewpidoodle Dog, shield sticker, circle patent sticker on back, stamped 3 on bottom, $1200-1500.

1.75" Kewpidoodle Dog and 2" Kewpie holding mandolin on 3.5" x 3.75" x 1.75" log planter, ©, 4882 or 4382, 53 on bottom of log, $2500-2800.

1.75" bisque Kewpidoodle Dog and 2" Kewpie Reader on 3.5" x 3.75" x 1.75" log planter, ©, incised 53, 4989, $2500-2800.

1.75" Kewpidoodle Dog attached to 3.25" x 1.75" wash tub with shamrocks, marked 6691, ©, $4000-4500; 2" bisque Kewpidoodle Dog by sunflower vase, ©, $4500-5000.

3.5" prone Kewpie with 1.75" Kewpidoodle Dog perched on back, incised O'Neill, ©, $1600-1800.

Chapter Two

Kewpie Dishes

In researching the Kewpie china patterns, only one ad was to be found. It was placed by Geo. Borgfeldt & Co., 16ᵗʰ Street, at Irving Place, New York, in the *Playthings* magazine of March 1914, which introduced Kewpie china and bisque novelties. "These are going to be all the rage this coming season—what mother could resist buying her child a KEWPIE CUP, SAUCER and PLATE, a PORRIDGE SET, a MUG or a BABY PLATE on which are the pictured KEWPIES?" The china shown in the ad is a Green Tree pattern plate, cup and saucer, and porridge set. The last paragraph reads, "The demand for these NOVELTIES has so far exceeded our expectations that we would strongly urge you to place your import order at once, to insure delivery." It would appear they were the rage and are still sought by Kewpie collectors all over the world.

For a presentation given at the Missouri affiliate meeting of the International Rose O'Neill Club (IROC), over fifty different Kewpie patterns or designs in adult, child, and doll china were found. All the German-made porcelain dishes used the same Kewpies decals. However, the mood of the artisan working that day determined the number and placement of the decals on the finished product. The large pieces generally have one of four large decals in the center with one or more of the twelve single Kewpie decals around the edge. Taller Kewpie pieces, such as the hatpin holder and the tall creamers, had a decal of a Kewpie cook standing on the back of another Kewpie.

There were factories all over Germany making Kewpie dishes for export. In the beginning of this chapter you will find examples of the different manufacturers' marks on Kewpie dishes. Some pieces made it through the line without being marked. Do not hesitate to buy an unmarked piece if the decals are authentic. There is one example included in this chapter showing reproduction decals. One look at these decals will tell you it is not a genuine Rose O'Neill creation.

After World War I broke out in Europe in 1914, Rose O'Neill and George F. Borgfeldt & Company had to turn to the American market to supply the demand for Kewpie dishes. Hence the introduction of Roma Pottery Co., East Liverpool, Ohio; Bennett SV, Baltimore, Maryland; H. Lerner Co., Brooklyn, New York; Holdfast, patented, D.E. McNicol, East Liverpool, Ohio; and The Pottery Co-operative Co., East Liverpool, Ohio.

The blue Jasperware Kewpie items were reproduced in blue and pink in the 1960s. The hatpin holder is marked Rose O'Neill Kewpie Germany, but was actually made in Japan. Those familiar with the Jasperware Kewpie pieces can readily see the difference. The reproductions are smaller and a lighter color blue. The original hatpin holder is 4.5" tall while the reproduction is only 4". The original cloverleaf dresser tray is 7" x 6.5" and the reproduction is 6" x 5.25". The original plaque measures 6" x 6.25" and reads "The Kewpies." The reproduction of this piece measures 5.75" x 6.25" and reads "The Kuties." The Ardalt Company of Japan also made fantasy pieces, which include a Kotton jar, Kosmetics jar, Koin Keeper, and Kandlelite holder.

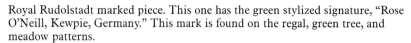

Left column, top to bottom:

This mark shows this piece to be copyrighted, "Rose O'Neill Wilson, Kewpie, Germany." The Royal Rudolstadt mark, as found on several different designs of Kewpie china, features a crown with a large "B" in a shield, Prussia across the top, and Royal Rudolstadt below. This mark is generally found on the tea pot and other large pieces. It would depend on the mood of the artisan working on the piece that day as to where this stamp was placed.

Royal Rudolstadt marked piece. This one has the green stylized signature, "Rose O'Neill, Kewpie, Germany." This mark is found on the regal, green tree, and meadow patterns.

Royal Rudolstadt marked piece. This one has the gold stylized signature, "Rose O'Neill, Kewpie, Germany."

Just the stylized signature, "Rose O'Neill, Kewpie, Germany." This mark was found on the green lustre and mushroom patterns.

Stylized signature, "Rose O'Neill Kewpie, England." Very rare.

"Copyrighted, Mrs. Rose O'Neill Wilson, Kewpies, Bavaria," is found on several different tea sets.

Many of the pieces only have "Bavaria" in gold, so don't pass up a Kewpie china piece because it doesn't have Rose's signature or copyright.

"Z.S. & Co." is the factory logo for the Zen, Scherzer & Company over Bavaria. It is found on many different china designs.

Right column, top to bottom:

The Z.S. & Co. logo is also found with a blue oval containing "Copyrighted, Mrs. Rose O'Neil Wilson, Kewpies." Note the one "l" in O'Neill.

Some pieces only have a gold oval with "Copyrighted, Mrs. Rose O'Neill Wilson, Kewpies."

The pink and green lustreware china came from the Leuchtenburg, Germany, company. Their logo features a castle turret with Leuchtenburg above and Germany below.

One of the Ohio pottery companies who started producing Kewpie dishes during World War I was "The Potters Co-operative Co., East Liverpool, Ohio, U.S.A." The flag over the circle logo reads semi-vitreous.

This mark is for the "Holdfast Baby Plate patented D.E. McNicol, East Liverpool, O."

"Bennett, S - V, Baltimore" was the mark of another manufacturer of Kewpie dishes for children.

The Roma Company was another pottery company in Ohio that made Kewpie youth and baby bowls and cups.

A Czechoslovakian pottery company produced a baby bowl, milk pitcher, and cup.

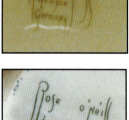

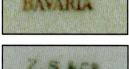

Regal pattern child's size dinner set. This pattern is cream colored with gold trimmed edge design, marked Prussia above a crown with a B in a crest and Royal Rudolstadt below, green stylized Rose O'Neill Wilson Kewpie Germany. 7" plates, $200-300; six cups and saucers (two not shown), 2" x 1.75" cups, $250-350; 4.25" saucers, $200-300; 3.25" x 3" sugar, $350-450; 5.75" x 2.75" teapot, $600-800; 3.25" x 2" creamer, $300-400.

Regal pattern footed bowl, gold trim with gold filigree design on back, Royal Rudolstadt, green stylized Rose O'Neill Kewpie Germany, 2.5" x 6"; six footed nut cups each marked Prussia above a crown with a B in a crest and Royal Rudolstadt below; Rose O'Neill Kewpie Germany, 1" x 2.75", set $2400-2600.

Bottom view of the Regal pattern footed bowl, showing the gold filigree design.

Adult size Regal pattern, marked Prussia above a crown with a B in a crest and Royal Rudolstadt below, Copyrighted Rose O'Neill Wilson Kewpie Germany, 4.25" x 4" sugar bowl, $325-425; 3.5" x 2.25" cup, $250-350; 6" saucer, $200-300; 3.5" x 3" creamer, $300-400.

Regal pattern, all pieces marked Prussia above a crown with a B in a crest and Royal Rudolstadt below; Copyrighted Rose O'Neill Wilson Kewpie Germany. Footed mayonnaise bowl, 2" x 4.5", $400-600; gold handle candy dish, 2.5" x 7.5", $500-700; hatpin holder, 5.25" x 2.75" base, $800-1000.

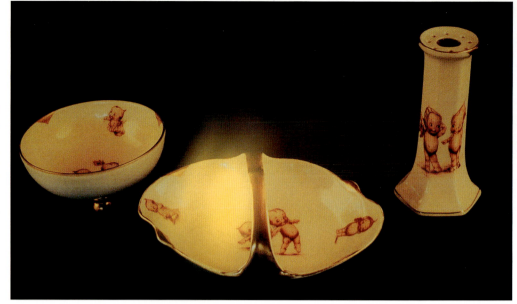

Regal pattern 10.5" handled serving plate, marked Prussia Royal Rudolstadt, $400-600; 7.5" footed bowl, Copyrighted, Rose O'Neill Wilson, Kewpie, Germany, $500-700.

Regal pattern, both pieces marked Prussia above a crown with a B in a crest and Royal Rudolstadt below; Copyrighted Rose O'Neill Wilson Kewpie Germany. Footed mayonnaise bowl, 2" x 4.5", $400-600; mayonnaise ladle, 5" long x 1.75" across bowl, $300-500.

Regal pattern toothpick holder, marked Prussia above a crown with a B in a crest, 2.25" x 2", $400-600; baby bowl, marked Prussia above a crown with a B in a crest and Royal Rudolstadt below, Copyrighted Rose O'Neill Wilson Kewpie Germany, 1.5" x 6.75", $600-800; jelly jar with spoon, marked Prussia above a crown with a B in a crest and Royal Rudolstadt below, 3.75" x 3" base, $800-1000.

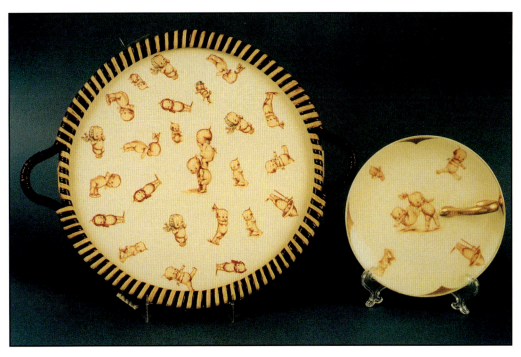

10.5" stoneware Kewpie tray mounted in a fiber tray with handles, marked 1913, 25, Rose O'Neill, Kewpie, Germany, $1200-1500; 6.5" Regal pattern bon-bon dish, marked Prussia above a crown with a B in a crest and Royal Rudolstadt below, Copyrighted Rose O'Neill Wilson Kewpie Germany, $700-900.

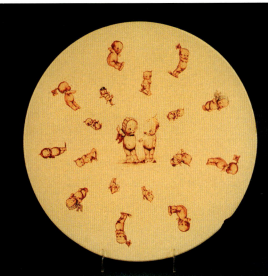

10.75" cream colored disk, .25" thick, green stylized Rose O'Neill Kewpie Germany, incised with 517, 87, and 1912. This piece may have been part of a dresser set with either a metal, wicker edge or fiber binding like the previous tray, $800-1000.

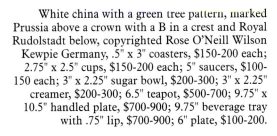

White china with a green tree pattern, marked Prussia above a crown with a B in a crest and Royal Rudolstadt below, copyrighted Rose O'Neill Wilson Kewpie Germany, .5" x 3" coasters, $150-200 each; 2.75" x 2.5" cups, $150-200 each; 5" saucers, $100-150 each; 3" x 2.25" sugar bowl, $200-300; 3" x 2.25" creamer, $200-300; 6.5" teapot, $500-700; 9.75" x 10.5" handled plate, $700-900; 9.75" beverage tray with .75" lip, $700-900; 6" plate, $100-200.

Adult size green tree pattern tea set, 6.25" cake plate, $100-200; 2.75" x 2.5" cup, $200-300; 5.25" saucer, $100-150; 3" x 3.25" sugar bowl, $225-325; 6.5" x 3.25" teapot, $500-700; 3.25" x 2.75" creamer, $225-325.

Green tree pattern hatpin holder, 5" x 2.5" base, $800-1000; egg cup, 2.5" x 1.75", $400-600; 5" x 7.25" metal basket, molded 1913, 7812, V10, stamped 3843, $800-1000; 3.25" x 3" sugar bowl with gold trim, marked NIH, $300-500; 5.75" x 2.75" teapot with gold trim, marked NIH, $700-900.

Green tree pattern trinket box, 1.75" x 3.75" x 2.75, $300-500; small pin tray, 3.75" x 5.5", $300-500; candy dish with handle, 4.25" x 6.75", $400-600.

Green tree pattern, markings: Kewpies, Mrs. Rose O'Neill Wilson, Kewpies, Germany. 6" dresser tray, $800-1000; three trinket jars with lids, one 3.5" and two 2.5" jars, $400-600 each; 5" hatpin holder, $800-1000.

Green tree pattern celery serving set, 6-sided star in relief on bottom, 5.75" x 12.5" server, $600-800; six 2.25" x 3.75" salt dips, $200-300 each.

Green tree pattern porridge set, 1.75" x 6.25" bowl, $200-300; 4" creamer, $250-350.

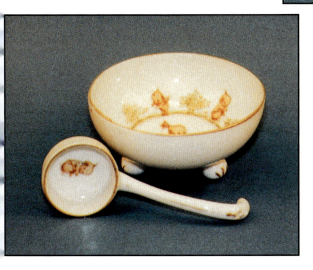

Green tree pattern footed mayonnaise bowl, 2" x 4.5", $400-600; mayonnaise ladle, 5" long x 1.75" across bowl, $300-500.

Four sizes of 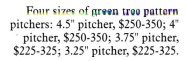 green tree pattern pitchers: 4.5" pitcher, $250-350; 4" pitcher, $250-350; 3.75" pitcher, $225-325; 3.25" pitcher, $225-325.

Different styles of green tree pattern cups: 3.5" x 2.25" cup, $200-300; 3.25" x 3.25" mug, $250-350; 3.25" x 3" adult cup, $200-300; 2.75" x 3.75" chocolate cup, $275-375; 2.75" x 2.5" child cup, $150-200; 3" x 1.75" child cup, $150-200.

Blue sky meadow pattern 6.25" plate, $100-200; 2.75" x 2.75" cup, $150-200; 5.25" saucer, $100-150; 3.25" x 2.75" creamer, $225-325.

Blue sky meadow pattern doll's 3.25" creamer, $225-325; child's 4" creamer, $250-350; 2.25" x 3.25" long trinket box, $300-500; 3.75" x 2.5" chocolate mug, $275-375; 1.5" x 3.5" strainer, $1000-1200; 2.75" x 1.5" salt and pepper, $800-1000.

Three sizes of blue sky meadow pattern plates: 8.5" plate, $150-250; 7.5" plate, $125-225; 7" plate, $100-200.

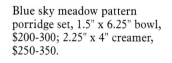

Blue sky meadow pattern porridge set, 1.5" x 6.25" bowl, $200-300; 2.25" x 4" creamer, $250-350.

Blue sky meadow pattern baby bowl, 1.5" x 7.75", $600-800; 1.25" x 7.5" bowl, $200-300.

2" x 7.5" handled warming baby dish in the blue sky meadow pattern, $600-800.

Blue sky meadow pattern celery dish with four salt dip servers. Celery dish, 12.5" x 6.5", $600-800; salt dips, 3.75" x 2.25", $200-300 each; 2" sterling salt spoons, Paye & Baker marking of three hearts, $100-150. Besides having Royal Rudolstadt markings, the celery dish also has a six pointed raised star on the bottom.

Blue sky meadow pattern 5.25" x 2.75" hatpin holder, $800-1000; 2" x 3.75" covered powder box, $500-700; 2.25" x 3.25" pin box, $300-500; 2" x 3.75" hair receiver, $500-700; 9.25" x 10.25" vanity tray, $600-800.

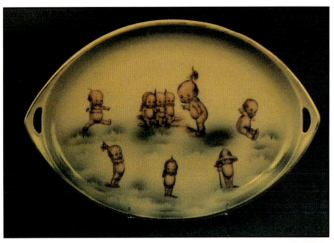

Yellow sky meadow pattern football-shaped, handled dish, 6.5" x 10", $600-800.

Yellow sky meadow pattern, marked in green, copyright, Rose O'Neill Wilson, Kewpie Germany, Royal Rudolstadt, 7" plate, $125-175; child's 1.5" x 7.75" feeding dish, $500-700; 2.5" x 2.75" cup, $150-250; 5" saucer, $100-200; 3.5" x 2.75" creamer, $300-400; 3" x 2.75" adult mug, $200-300; 2.25" x 3.5" cup, $200-300; 6" saucer, $150-250.

6" yellow sky meadow pattern cake plates, $1000-1200 set.

Two 4" white china saucers, action Kewpies with Prussian type helmets and swords added, marked Miami Doll Club, 1961, May Hausen, $75-125 each; 2.5" x 2.75" yellow sky meadow pattern Prussian Soldier cups, $200-300 each; 5.25" saucer, $150-250.

Child's green lustreware Prussian Soldier tea set with embossed beading around scalloped edges, marked Leuchtenburg, Germany, 3.5" creamer, $300-400; 3.5" sugar bowl, $300-400; 2" x 2" cups, $150-200; 4.5" saucers, $50-75 each; 5.5" teapot, $400-600. This set is also found in pink lustreware.

Child's green lustreware set with embossed beading around scalloped edges, marked Leuchtenburg, Germany, 2" x 2" cups, $100-150; 4.5" saucer, $50-75; 3.5" sugar bowl, $250-350; 3.5" creamer, $250-350; 5.5" teapot, $350-550; 5.25" cake plate, $200-300.

Four pieces of Prussian Kewpie Soldiers with ladder at window pattern, 6" plate, $300-400; 3" x 2.5" creamer, $350-450; 7" plate, $300-400; 6.25" bowl, $400-500.

Eloping Kewpies pattern 1.75" x 6.5" bowl, marked #1, $300-400; adult size bowl, 1.25" x 8.25", $350-450; 2.75" x 2.75" cup, $300-400; two 6" plates, $250-350 each.

Leaning tree pattern beverage tray and coaster set, .75" x 9.75" beverage tray, $700-900; coasters, .5" x 2.75", $150-200 each.

Leaning tree pattern 6.25" bon-bon dish with handle, marked in green, Rose O'Neill, Kewpie, Germany, Royal Rudolstadt, $700-900; 3.75" x 2.75" jelly jar, marked the same as bon-bon dish, $800-1000.

Leaning tree pattern handled serving plate, 9.75" x 10.5", $400-600.

Child's pink lustreware with embossed beading around scalloped edges, marked Leuchtenburg, Germany, 2" x 2" cups, $100-150; 4.5" saucer, $50-75; 3.5" sugar bowl, $250-350; 3.5" creamer, $250-350; 5.5" teapot, $350-550; 5.25" cake plates, $200-300.

Child's white china with embossed beading around scalloped edges, marked Leuchtenburg, Germany, 2" x 2" cups, $100-150; 4.5" saucer, $50-75; 3.5" sugar bowl, $250-350; 3.5" creamer, $250-350; 5.5" teapot, $350-550; 5.25" cake plates, $200-300.

Child's pink shaded daisy pattern lustreware with embossed beading around scalloped edges, marked Leuchtenburg, Germany, 2" x 2" cups, $100-150; 3.5" sugar bowl, $250-350; 3.5" creamer, $250-350; 5.5" teapot, $350-550; 5.25" cake plates, $200-300.

Child's gray lustreware with stenciled fern pattern and embossed beading around scalloped edges, marked Leuchtenburg, Germany, 2" x 2" cups, $100-150; 3.5" sugar bowl, $250-350; 3.5" creamer, $250-350; 5.5" teapot, $350-550; 5.25" cake plates, $200-300.

Three-color stenciled fern pattern embossed china, marked Leuchtenburg, Germany, 2.5" x 3" adult cup, $150-250; 5" saucer, $75-125; 3.5" sugar bowl, $250-350; 2.75" x 2.5" creamer, $250-350; 5.5" teapot, $350-550; 7" plates, $200-300.

Three-color stenciled fern pattern embossed china, marked Leuchtenburg, Germany, 2.25" x 5" berry bowl, $200-300; 2.5" x 3" adult cup, $150-250; 3.75" x 2.75" chocolate cup, $275-375; 2.5" x 2.5" child's cup, $100-200; 2.25" x 2.25" child's cup, $100-200; 8.25" plates, $200-300 each.

Stenciled fern pattern 5.5" x 6.5" pitcher, $400-500; 2.5" x 8.25" bowl, $200-300; both marked Rose O'Neill Kewpie Germany in green.

Stenciled fern pattern 11.25" x 10.5" handled plate, marked Rose O'Neill Kewpie Germany in green, $600-800.

Three-color stenciled fern pattern embossed lustreware, marked Leuchtenburg, Germany, 1.5" x 7" baby dish, $500-700; 3.25" x 3" creamer, $200-300.

Stenciled fern-leaf lustreware two-piece covered butter dish, 8.25" plate with 6" domed cover, both pieces marked Rose O'Neill Kewpie Germany, $1000-1200.

3.75" x 4" stenciled fern-leaf lustreware huge cup, marked Rose O'Neill Kewpie Germany, $300-400.

Green leaf pattern, child's creamer, 3.5" x 2.25", $300-400; two 1.75" x 2.25" trinket boxes, Kewpie on lid only, $200-300; child's 2.5" x 2.75" cup, $150-200; 4.5" saucer, $150-200; 3" x 3.25" sugar bowl, $400-500; 2.75" x 2.25" trinket jar, $300-400; 7" plate, $200-300; child's 2" x 2.25" cup, $150-200; 3.25" x 1.75" creamer, $300-400.

White embossed swirl tea set with gold trim, marking #4, 2" x 2.25" cup, $125-225; 4.25" saucer, $100-200; 3.75" x 3.25" sugar, $250-350; 6" x 4" teapot, $400-600; 2.75" x 2.5" creamer, $250-350; 5.25" plate, $125-225.

Child's embossed tea set with gold wreaths, markings #3 and #4, 2" x 2.25" cup, $125-225; 4.25" saucer, $100-200; 3.25" x 3.75" sugar, $250-350; 3.75" x 5" teapot, $350-550; 5.25" plate, $125-225; 2.5" x 2.75" creamer, $250-350.

Green lustre shading with gold trim and wreaths, 2.5" x 2.5" child's cup, $150-250; 4.75" saucer, $100-200; 7.5" plate, $200-300; 3.25" x 3.5" adult creamer, $250-350; 1.25" x 5.75" bowl, $200-300.

Gold wreath pattern with lavender shading, 3" x 3.5" x 3.75" adult creamer, $250-350.

Child's white china tea set with gold trim on embossed beading around scalloped edges, 2" x 2" cups, $100-150; 4.25" saucer, $100-150; 3.5" sugar bowl, $250-350; 3.5" creamer, $250-350; 5.5" teapot, $350-450.

Multi-floral border pattern, marked Z.S. & Co., Bavaria, Mrs. Rose O'Neill Wilson, Kewpie, 3.25" x 2.75" child size sugar bowl, $250-350; 2.5" x 2" creamer, $200-300; 2" x 3.75" trinket box, $300-500; three 5" saucers, $150-250 each; 2.25" x 2.75" cup, $200-300; 7.5" plate, $250-350; 1.25" x 5.25" dessert bowl, $200-300; 6" plate, $250-350; adult size, 2.5" x 2.75" cup, $200-300; adult size, 2.75" x 3.75" creamer, $200-300.

Multi-floral border pattern, marked Z.S. & Co., Bavaria, Mrs. Rose O'Neill Wilson, Kewpie, 10.5" sandwich plate, $600-800; 2.75" x 3.75" creamer, $200-300; six 2.5" cups and 5" saucers, $350-400 each.

12" x 5.25" oval celery dish, multi-floral border pattern, marked Z.S. & Co., Bavaria, Mrs. Rose O'Neill Wilson, Kewpie, $600-800; 3.75" x 2.25" salt server, $200-300.

Gold border with dropped ringlet, 12.25" x 5.25" celery bowl, $600-800; 5" hatpin holder, marked 8880, $800-1000; 7" plate, $200-300; 2.25" x 2.75" cup and 5.75" saucer, $350-400; 5.5" x 3.5" pin tray, $150-250.

Royal pattern, soft ivory color with elaborate gold trim,
4.5" sugar bowl, $300-400; 4.5" creamer, $300-400; 5.5"
biscuit jar, $2500-3000; 12.5" large cake plate or tray,
$600-800.

Royal pattern, soft ivory color with elaborate gold
trim, 2.5" x 4.25" hair receiver, $600-800.

White china with fruit and foliage pattern around top and edge of lids, 5.5" biscuit jar, $2500-3000; 10" chocolate pot, $800-1000.

Fruit and foliage border pattern, 5.5" bon-bon dish, 2" high with handle, marked Copyright Mrs. Rose O'Neill Wilson Kewpies in blue lustre stamp on bottom, $700-900; 5.25" x 4" candy/nut basket server, marked Z.S & Co., Bavaria, $800-1000.

Green lattice border design with floral accents, 2.5" x 3" unusual shaped cup, $250-350; 6" cake plate, $200-300; 3.75" sugar bowl, $250-350; 2.25" x 3.5" cup, $200-300; 6" saucer, $175-275.

Gold laurel with gray shading over Kewpies, marked in gold, copyright Mrs. Rose O'Neill Wilson, Kewpies, Bavaria, 2.25" x 3.5" adult cup, $150-250; 5.75" saucer, $100-200; 9.5" serving plate with notches, $300-400; 7.5" plate, $150-250; child's 4.75" saucer, $100-200.

Rose garden pattern with pink and yellow roses border, marked Z.S. & Co. Bavaria, Copyrighted Mrs. Rose O'Neill Wilson, Kewpies, 2.75" x 3.5" sugar bowl, $150-250 without lid, $250-350 with lid; 5" saucer, $125-175; 4" x 3" chocolate cup, $275-375; 2.25" x 2.5" cup, $200-300; 3" x 3.25" creamer, $200-300.

Child size Kewpies, sailing pattern sugar bowl, 3" x 3.25", $400-500; trinket box, 1.25" x 2.25", $300-400; creamer, 3.25" x 1.75", $300-400.

Kewpie sailing pattern, Royal Rudolstadt, Copyrighted, Rose O'Neill Wilson, Kewpies, Germany, 5.5" plate, $250-350; 2.5" cup, $250-350.

Kewpie tight-rope walker pattern 3" x 3.5" creamer, marked #1, $300-400; 1.75" x 7" baby dish, $700-900; 2" x 3.25" cup, $200-300; 5.5" saucer, $100-150.

Blue sky meadow pattern with goose baby bowl, 1.5" x 7.75", $800-1000; footed hair receiver, 3.5" x 4", $700-900; footed powder box, 3.5" x 4", $700-900.

Child tea set size cups and saucers in matching gold pinwheel floral design, cups, 2.5" x 2.75", $150-250 each; 5" saucers, $100-200 each.

10" x 7.5" gold lacy-bordered dresser tray with roses and Kewpies, Copyright Mrs. Rose O'Neill Wilson Kewpie, Z.S. & Co., Bavaria, 8882, $800-1000.

6.5" gold lacy-bordered plate with roses and Kewpies, Copyright Mrs. Rose O'Neill Wilson Kewpie, Z.S. & Co., Bavaria, 8882, $300-400.

8.25" x 2.25" gold tasseled pattern bowl, Rose O'Neill Kewpies, Germany, Bavaria, $300-400.

Gold tasseled pattern 3" x 4" adult creamer, Bavaria, $250-350.

Gold scrolling with four-leaf clovers in circles, handled relish dish; 8.25" x 4.75", marked Royal Munich, 8868, Z.S. & Co. over Bavaria, $400-600.

Lavender flowers with gold arch over Kewpies, 2.5" x 9" serving bowl, marking #4, $300-400.

Lavender shading gold arch cup, Copyrighted Mrs. Rose O'Neill Wilson, Kewpies, Bavaria, 2.5" x 2.75", $150-250; 7.5" plate, gold filigree around outer edge with gold inner trim, marked Z.S. & Co., Bavaria, $200-300; 6" plate with gold rim, Thomas, Bavaria, $150-250.

Mushroom pattern trivet, 5.75" x .5" thick, $400-600; possible dresser set holder, 10" x .25" thick, incised 1913/25, stamped 3841, Rose O'Neill Germany, $600-800; tea strainer and holder, 1.5" x 3.5" x 5.5" strainer, $1000-1200.

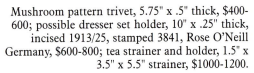

7.5" gold edged rim using decal of three Kewpies with added Prussian helmets and swords, one of four different designed plates, marked Royal Bayreuth, Bavaria, $400-600.

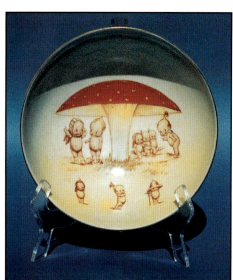

Mushroom pattern 3.75" x 8.5" footed bowl, $600-800.

Marking and round gold feet of previous bowl.

6" green lattice border pattern dish, marked Z.S. & Co., Mrs. Rose O'Neill Wilson, $250-350.

Alphabet baby bowl, 1.75" x 6.75", $600-800; 7.5" plate, $400-600; 6.75" plate, $300-500; 2" x 2" child's cup, $300-500.

Holdfast alphabet baby plate, 1.75" deep x 8.25", $300-400.

3.5" x 3.75" milk glass child's cups, $150-200 each; 8.5" milk glass baby bowls, marked Kewpie Trademark, copyright 1920, By Rose O'Neill Wilson, $250-350 each.

1.25" x 7.5" yellow lustreware baby bowl, no marking, $250-350; child's red trimmed 1" x 6.75" pottery baby bowl, no marking, $250-350.

2" x 5.25" child's bowls, marked Roma, $150-250.

Baby warming bowls with handles and spout, 2.25" x 7.75", marked Excello Trademark 1700, $400-500; 2" x 6.25", marked H. Lerner Co., Brooklyn, NY, $300-400.

Divided baby bowl, 2.25" x 6.75", marked chromium, made in USA, Bakelite handles and cap cover, $400-500; 2.5" x 6", marked Excello Trademark, $300-400.

Lavender handled baby warming bowl, H & Co., Bavaria, 1.75" x 5.5" not including spout, $400-500; hand painted baby bowl, 2" x 5.5", made in Czechoslovakia, $250-350; milk pitcher, 3.75" x 2.5" not including handle, made in Czechoslovakia, $300-500.

Child's divided plates, colors vary from light ivory to yellow, marked Roma, 7.5" cream colored plate, $200-300; 2.75" x 2.75" yellow cup, $250-350; 7.5" yellow colored plate, $200-300; 7.5" ivory colored plate, $200-300.

The Pottery Company gold trimmed porridge set, .25" x 5.75" bowl, $300-400; 3.5" x 3.25" milk pitcher, $200-300.

Reproduction cup and saucer, poor quality Kewpie decals, not marked, 2" x 2.5" cup and 5" saucer. We are showing these to make you aware that there are reproductions of Kewpie china.

Child's cream with red band trim tea set, marked Bennett S-V Baltimore on plates, 1.5" x 1.75" cup, $100-150; 2.75" saucer, $75-125; 1.75" x 2.25" sugar, $150-250; 4.75" x 3" teapot, $250-350; 2.25" x 2.25" creamer, $100-200.

Twenty-three piece set of blue sky with brown shading miniature dishes in box, marked Kewpie Germany, 2.75" teapot, 2.5" sugar bowl, 2.25" saucers, 1.25" cups, 2.5" plates, $1800-2200.

Child's tea set in box, "Toy tea set, made in Germany" on box, teapot marked Rose O'Neill, Kewpie, England, two cups, two saucers, sugar bowl, teapot, creamer, and two lids, $1400-1600.

Blue sky with brown shading 1" x 1.5" x 1.5" dresser box, 2" chamber pot, 3" pitcher and 5" bowl, one dresser box missing, $1200-1500.

Blue sky with brown shading 1" covered tooth-brush holder, 1" covered soap dish, 3" chamber pot, 5" pitcher in bowl, $1600-1800.

103

Child's tea set with green grass and blue sky, 2.5" x 2.75" creamer, $150-250; 3.5" x 3.75" teapot, $300-400; 3.25" x 3.25" sugar bowl, $200-300; 1.75" x 2" cup, $75-125; 3.5" saucer, $50-100.

Child's brown shading with blue sky tea set, 1.75" x 2" cup, $100-150; 3.25" saucer, $75-125; 2.25" x 2.5" sugar (pictured without lid), with lid $200-300; 2.5" x 3.75" teapot, $250-350; 2" x 2.25" creamer, $100-200.

Child's brown shading with blue sky tea set, 1.75" x 2" cup, $100-150; 3.25" saucer, $75-125; 2.25" x 2.5" sugar, $200-300; 2.5" x 3.75" teapot, $250-350; 4" cake plate, $100-150; 2" x 2.25" creamer, $100-200.

Doll size, twenty-three piece set includes 4" teapot, 2.5" sugar bowl, 2" creamer in moon silhouette with blue shading, marked Rose O'Neill Kewpie Germany, $1600-1800.

Child's orange trimmed dinner set (all pieces not shown), includes cup, 1.5" x 3"; 5" plates; 6" keyhole handled cake plate; gravy boat, 2" x 5.25" x 3.25"; sugar, 2.25" x 2.5" not including handles; creamer, 2" x 2.25"; teapot, 3.5"; platter, 5.25" x 3.25"; covered casserole bowl, 3.75" x 6.25" including handles x 4"; made in Japan, $800-1000.

Child's gold lustre tea set, made in Japan, 1.25" x 2.5" cup, $25-50; 3.5" saucer, $25-50; 1.25" x 2.25" cup, $25-50; 3.25" saucer, $25-50; 2.5" x 1.75" sugar, $75-100; 3.5" x 2.75" teapot, $100-150; 1.75" x 1.50" creamer, $75-100; 5" notched cake plate, $50-100. Also shown is gray lustre child's tea set, 2.25" x 1.75" creamer, $75-100; 1.25" saucer, $25-50; 4.25" plate, $50-75; 2" x 2" sugar (pictured without lid), with lid $75-100.

Shepherd of the Hills doll tea set, 1.25" creamer, 2.25" plate, 2.25" x 3" teapot, 1" x 1.25" cup, 1.75" x 1.25" sugar, $50-100.

Four piece red tin doll tea set, 3" plate, 2.75" x 2" base teapot, cups 1.5" x 1.75" rim, $1200-1400.

105

Three piece tin doll tea set, 2.75" x 2" base teapot, cups 1.5" x 1.75" rim, $1000-1200.

Blue enamelware bowl, 1" x 7.25", $100-150; blue enamelware cup, 2.75" x 3", $100-150; yellow child's enamelware bowl, 1.25" x 5.5", $200-300; yellow child's enamelware cup, 2.5" x 2.5", $200-300. If the blue set were in better condition, it would bring the same price as the yellow set.

2.5" x 3" and 3.75" x 2.75" lithophane cups in brown tones, Kewpie farmer in cameo type pink frame, Royal Bayreuth trademarks, $1000-1200 each.

Bottom of previous brown tone lithophane cup.

2.5" x 3" lithophane cup in green tones, black handle and rim, Kewpie farmer in cameo type pink frame, Royal Bayreuth trademark, $1000-1200.

Engraved silver nursery pieces marked M over a cutlass, sterling; three applied Kewpies on P & B marked cup, 1.75" x 2.5", engraved Jack, $200-300; four Kewpies engraved on 2.75" x 3" cup, marked A2300 from C & H, 1914, $200-300; four Kewpies engraved on 2.25" x 3" cup, marked 307, $200-300; engraved bowl, 2" x 4.5", marked 132, 19/31, $250-350; handled bowl, engraved John Henry Vought III, 2-5-1921, marked 132-1, $300-400.

The following pieces appear to be early china painting craft projects. 3.75" x 4.5" trinket box, marked Limoges, France, DePose Trademark C/M in triangle, $150-200; 2.75" x 2.75" cup, inscribed on bottom, To Hazel from Aunt Gertie, 1914, C.T. Altwasser, Silesia Trademark, $75-125; 2.75" x 4.5" footed powder box, initialed EML, MZ Austria Trademark, $100-150; 4" x 3.5" powder dispenser, marked PL, Limoges, France Trademark, $50-100; 3.5" x 3.5" mug, 2.5" at opening, Belleck-Willets, initialed A.R., $75-125; 7.5" plate, TAV Limoges, France, inscribed Xmas 1915, Eldreith, artist, M. Trezise, $75-125; 4.5" x 2.25" powder shaker, KC Royal Bavaria, pat. applied for, Trademark, $100-125; 3.5" x 1.25" salt shaker, pearlized finish, Nippon, $50-75; 4.75" x 2.5" x 1.5" powder shaker, green crown and marking, artist MB, $100-125.

Blue Jasperware clocks, made in Germany by Schaffer & Vater of Rudolstadt, Thuringia, Germany; all are marked Copyrighted Rose O'Neill Germany, 4" x 5" arched clock with two Kewpies, $300-500; 4" x 5" domed table clock with two Kewpies, $300-500; 3.5" x 4.75" tall clock with two Kewpies, floral accents, and butterflies, $300-500; 5.75" x 6" cathedral clock with three Kewpies, floral garland accent, $400-600; 5.75" x 6" arched mantle clock with four Kewpies and a floral swag, $400-600.

Schaffer & Vater blue Jasperware pieces, 2.5" x 3" hair receiver, $250-300; 4.5" hatpin holder, $700-800; 2.5" x 3.5" heart shaped covered trinket jar, $400-450; 2.75" x 3.25" round powder jar, $300-400; 6" round plate with border and "The Kewpies" on bow, $300-350; 4.5" round planter with ceramic liner, $300-350; 3.5" x 4" sugar bowl and lid, $250-300; 3.5" x 2.5" tall round covered jar, $300-400; 4.5" x 3.5" curved pin tray, $300-350; 2.5" x 3.5" creamer, $175-225; 4" milk pitcher, $250-300; 7" cloverleaf dresser tray, $400-500; 1.75" x 3.5" vase, $300-400; 8.5" bud base, $400-500.

Green Jasperware pieces, made in Germany by Schaffer & Vater; all are marked Copyrighted Rose O'Neill Germany, 2.5" x 3.5" heart shaped covered trinket jar, $400-450; 3.5" x 4.75" tall clock with two Kewpies, $300-500; 4" x 5" arched clock with two Kewpies, $300-500; 5.75" x 5.75" arched clock with four Kewpies and a floral swag, $400-600; 1.75" x 3.5" vase, $300-400; 4" x 4.5" triangular wall hanger with three seated Kewpies, $300-400; 6" round plate with border and "The Kewpies" on bow, $300-350; 3" x 4" sugar bowl and lid, $250-300; 2.5" x 3.5" creamer, $175-225; 4" milk pitcher, $250-300; 3.5" x 2.5" round covered jar, $300-400; 8.5" bud base, $400-500.

Metal Kewpie Items

Rose O'Neill was known to be a chain smoker, so it is understandable that she would establish a relationship with Louis V. Aronson to make her metal Kewpie pieces. Louis V. Aronson, inventor and patent holder for the safety match, founded the Ronson Company. He also invented the first pocket lighter in 1913.

Aronson was born on December 25, 1869. In 1883, he joined a technical high school in New York where he specialized in small metal art objects. During his studies, he invented and registered his first patent, the electro-plating of metal. With this method it was possible to coat metal with chrome or gold plating by electrons. His method is still used today. To raise capital to establish his Art Metal Company, Aronson sold his patent to several companies.

In 1897, the prosperous company moved from New York to Newark, New Jersey and the name was changed to Art Metal Works. They manufactured various art and home decoration products, such as clocks, vases, desk sets, miniatures, and many other novelties useful for wedding and holiday gifts.

The Art Metal Works name can be found on a few of the Kewpie pieces shown in this chapter. It is believed they were the primary manufacturer of these items.

Paye & Baker Manufacturing Company (P & B) is best known for its sterling souvenir spoons. This company was formed when Frank Baker bought out Jessie Simmons from the firm of Simmons & Baker in 1901. Paye & Baker manufactured most of the metal Kewpie novelty items. Their trademark consisted of three linking hearts. The first heart contained a "P", the middle heart contained an ampersand ("&"), and the last heart contained a "B".

There are many reproduction pewter Kewpie pieces available. They lack the quality and trademark of the pieces made by Art Metal Works or the Paye & Baker Manufacturing Company.

12.5" metal lamp with shade, 9" x 8" lamp base with two 4.25" kicking Kewpies leaning against lamp post, $1800-2200.

4.5" kicking Kewpie, 10.5" tall, tapered fluted column with rose, inverted tulip chain on 4.75" round base, marked AMW, Newark, NJ, made in USA, $1200-1400.

Bottom of lamp at right, with Art Metal Works, Newark, NJ, made in USA, incised on base.

Left: 6.5" Kewpie Thinker on 10.75" lamp with 5.25" x 6" base, $1500-1800.

Right: 11" lamp with 6.5" Kewpie Thinker on 5.5" embossed base, $1500-1800.

10" high lamp with 6" standing Kewpie, socket for lamp extending from head, banister between two posts, $1800-2000.

9.5" lamp with 4.25" seated Kewpie on 6" x 8" base, four floral groupings on base, $1400-1600.

9.5" lamp, same as previous lamp with lace covered lamp shade, $1400-1600.

Pair of 9" metal lamps, each with 3.75" standing Kewpie with arms back, fluted column, two laurel wreaths on 4.25" base, $1200-1400.

9" lamp has 3.75" standing Kewpie with arms back, ornate column on 4.25" base, $1400-1600.

10.75" lamp with 6" standing Kewpie on decorative floral 4" x 4.75" base, $1400-1600.

10.5" stripped lamp with 4.25" Thinker Kewpie on 5.5" base, $1000-1200; 9" lamp with 4.5" repainted kicker Kewpie on 6" base, $1200-1400.

12.25" lamp with 6.5" bronze Scootles on 3.5" base, $1000-1200.

11" lamp with 4.25" kicking Kewpie on 3" base, petaled column top, $1200-1400.

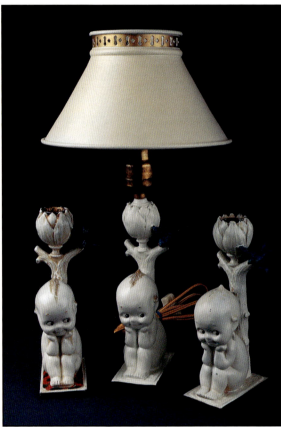

Kewpie Trademark Thinker candlesticks with bluebird on tree branch, tulip shaped candle holder, 7.5" with 4.75" Thinker, base 2.25" x 4", $1000-1200 each; Thinker lamp with bluebird on tree branch, tulip shaped receptacle holder, $1200-1400.

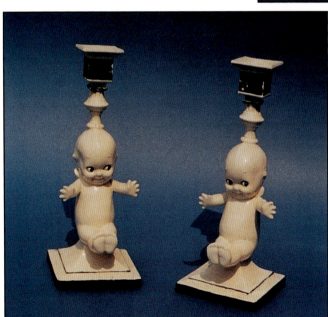

4.5" seated Kewpies on 8.25" candlesticks with 3" square base, $1200-1400 each.

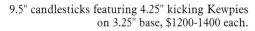

9.5" candlesticks featuring 4.25" kicking Kewpies on 3.25" base, $1200-1400 each.

9.25" white metal candlestick, 4.25" kicking Kewpie on 3.5" x 3.5" base with green trim, $1200-1400; 4.5" white metal candleholder, 4.25" kicking Kewpie on 3.5" base, $1200-1400.

2.5" x 2.75" Blunderboo Kewpie on 2.25" x 4.25" base with 2.75" candlestick, marked des. pat. 43860, Kewpie Trademark, $1000-1200.

Three piece matching metal planter and candlestick arrangement, 3.75" x 13.5" planter with two 2.75" standing Kewpies, $1400-1600; 9.5" x 4.25" base candlesticks with 4" kneeling Kewpies, $1400-1600.

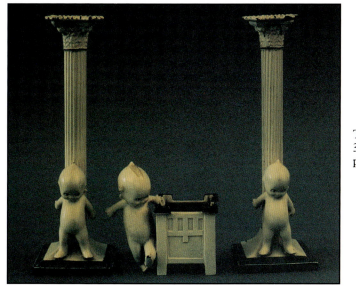

Two 9.5" candlesticks, each with a 4" Kewpie standing on 3.25" x 3.25" base, $1200-1400 each; 4.25" kicking Kewpie with 2.5" square planter in white metal, $1400-1600.

Two 5" Kewpies standing beside a 9" planter with removable tin liner, embossed Kewpie Trademark, $1800-2000.

4.25" kicking Kewpie on 4.5" x 6" jewelry box, marked design patent, Kewpie Trademark, $1800-2000; 9.5" candlestick with 4.25" kicking Kewpie on 3.25" square base, $1000-1200.

9.75" candlestick holder on 4.25" base with 3.75" kneeling Kewpie, $1200-1400; 5.5" x 6.75" x 4.5" jewelry box with 2.5" Blunderboo Kewpie, $1800-2000; 6.75" bud vase with 4.5" kicking Kewpie on 2.5" base, $1000-1200.

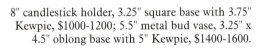

8" candlestick holder, 3.25" square base with 3.75" Kewpie, $1000-1200; 5.5" metal bud vase, 3.25" x 4.5" oblong base with 5" Kewpie, $1400-1600.

8" double candleholders with 2" Kewpie sitting on center column, $1800-2000.

5" Kewpie standing between uneven bud vases, 5.75" and 7" columns, bluebird on 3" x 4.25" base, $1200-1400; 4" kicking Kewpie between two bud vases, 6" and 8" columns, 3" x 4.5" floral and shell patterned base, $1000-1200

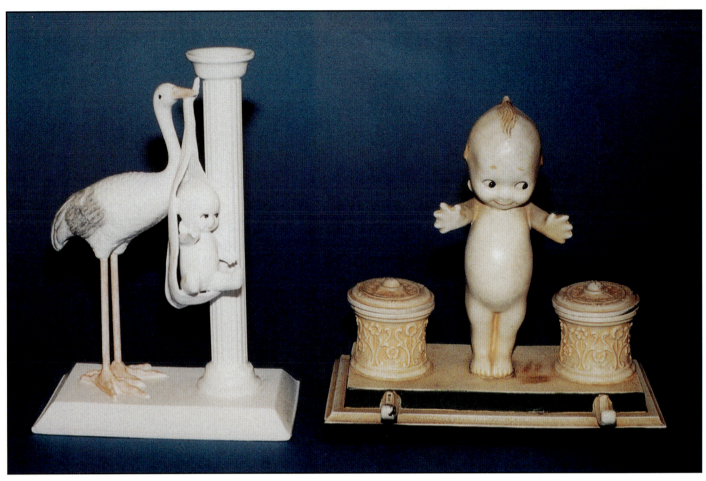

6.75" bud vase on 2.5" x 4.75" base, 5.75" stork holding 2" baby Kewpie, $1800-2200; 6" double inkwell, 6.25" x 3" base with 5" standing Kewpie, $2000-2400.

4.5" Thinker Kewpie sitting beside inkwell with lid and glass insert, embossed with des. pat. 43860 and Kewpie Trademark, $1800-2000.

3" Blunderboo Kewpie on 4.5" x 6" base beside hinged inkwell with porcelain insert, embossed Kewpie Trademark and des. pat. 43860, $1800-2000.

7.5" x 10" hinged metal jewelry box with one 3.5" crawling Kewpie and one 4" kneeling Kewpie, painted red roses, $2000-2400.

Bon-Bon dish on pedestal, 5.25" x 5", with 2" Kewpie, marked des. pat. 43860, Kewpie Trademark, $900-1100; trinket box, 4.75" x 5", with 2" Kewpie, marked des. pat. 43860, Kewpie Trademark, $1400-1600; candlestick (upper part of candlestick missing) with 4" kneeling Kewpie, marked des. pat. 43860, Kewpie Trademark, base 2.25" x 2.25", $800-1000, as shown.

4" kneeling Kewpie on 4.5" square embossed hinged box, 6.5" overall height, Trademark and des. pat. 43860, $1600-1800.

2" seated Kewpie on 2" x 4.5" white stamp box, hinged top, $1400-1600.

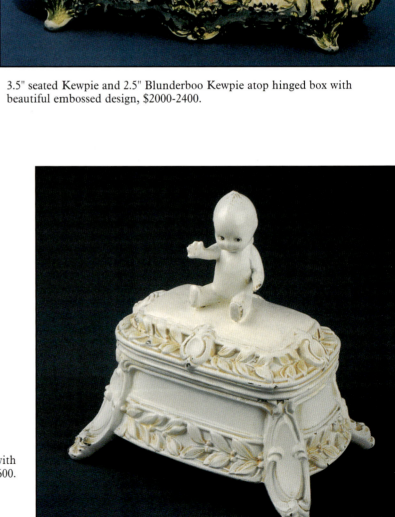

3.5" seated Kewpie and 2.5" Blunderboo Kewpie atop hinged box with beautiful embossed design, $2000-2400.

Large jewelry box, 4.5" x 6.5" x 10.5", with 3.75" Kewpie leaning against gold design filigree, $2000-2400.

2" seated Kewpie atop 5" x 5" x 3" jewelry box with silk lining, embossed markings, $1400-1600.

White metal trinket box, 5" x 5" x 3.5", with 3" Blunderboo Kewpie, Kewpie Trademark, $1400-1600; white metal calendar holder, 6.75" x 4.5", with "O" mouth upright crawling Kewpie, $2600-3000.

4.5" kicking Kewpie with calendar, 1.25" glass ink bottle with metal lid, and pen holder, 6.25" overall height, Kewpie Trademark on back, $2500-3000.

4.5" kicking Kewpie brass picture frame, stripped of original finish, 9.5" x 5.25", $1000-1200.

Painted metal dresser mirror, 10.5" x 5.75", with 4" kneeling Kewpie on 3.25" square base, des. patent Kewpie Trademark, $2600-3000.

4" "O" mouth Kewpie atop 5.5" x 9.5" picture frame, $1800-2000.

Three raised Kewpies on 7.25" x 5.5" picture frame with picture of Rose O'Neill, $800-1000.

8" metal bookends with Thinker Kewpies seated on 3.75" x 5.25" book base, $1400-1600 each.

2" seated Kewpie atop metal clock, 1.5" x 3" x 6" overall, $2800-3000.

13" cast iron full body Kewpie doorstop, $1000-1200; 13" brass Thinker Kewpie, $1400-1600; 14" cast iron half body Kewpie door-stop, $1000-1200.

13" cast iron Kewpie andirons, $1200-1500.

3" cast iron Thinker Kewpies, $150-200 each.

6" metal Kewpie mascot on 2" base, with arms extended, holding gold tassels, $2400-2600.

123

4.5" brass Kewpie without wings on knock-off radiator cap, $400-500; 5" chrome plated Kewpie with wings on .75" base mounted on radiator cap with wings, $500-600; 4" brass Kewpie clown on dog bone radiator cap, $300-400.

6" white metal Kewpie with Kewpie Trademark on radiator cap with accessory for four flags clamped on 8" wings, $2500-2700.

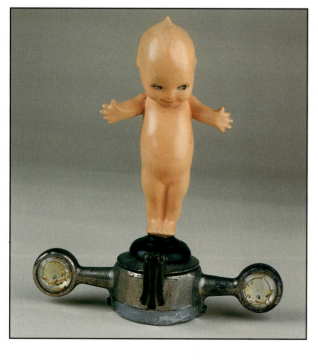

6" painted Kewpie with Kewpie Trademark, same as one before but painted in flesh tones, 7.5" wide radiator cap, glass-eyed with Kewpie picture inside, $2000-2200.

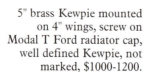

5" brass Kewpie mounted on 4" wings, screw on Modal T Ford radiator cap, well defined Kewpie, not marked, $1000-1200.

6" chrome plated Kewpie with embossed Kewpie Trademark, reg US pat off, © ROW inside heart, mounted on ornate brass 12.25" wing span radiator cap, marked RYO patented, turning wings allows water to be added without removing cap, $2000-2200.

4.75" chrome plated over brass Kewpie, no wings, $300-400; 6" Kewpie with wings, brass with plating, marked Kewpie reg US pat off © ROW inside a heart, on dog bone radiator cap, top knot flattened, plating rough, $1600-1800; 4" brass chrome plated Kewpie with wings from Australia, on a radiator cap with wings, $600-800.

5" white metal Thinker Kewpie on 13.75" brass wings, mound base made to mount on radiator cap by Art Metal Works, Reg Pat 43860, Trademark Kewpie, $1800-2000.

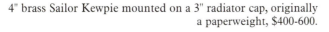

4" brass Sailor Kewpie mounted on a 3" radiator cap, originally a paperweight, $400-600.

6" aluminum Kewpie, possible older reproduction from Art Metal Works, marked Kewpie on back, on chrome plated Model T Ford radiator cap, $800-1000.

7.25" cast aluminum winged Kewpie with moveable arms, obtained from Santiago, Chile, 9.25" wing span, chrome wing on brass radiator cap, $600-800.

5.25" cast iron Kewpie with wings on heart shaped base, mounted on 6" wide brass dog bone radiator cap, $400-600.

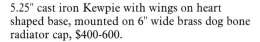

5.25" Kewpie holding wiener over head, purportedly recovered from Bonniebrook after the fire, mounted on 7" wing span screw on radiator cap, $600-800.

5.5" aluminum Kewpie with wings on chrome plated 6" wide dog bone radiator cap, $400-600.

5" aluminum Kewpie with wings on streamlined winged radiator cap, $600-800.

4.25" metal Kewpie standing on ball, $150-250; 7" metal Kewpie paperweight, $200-400.

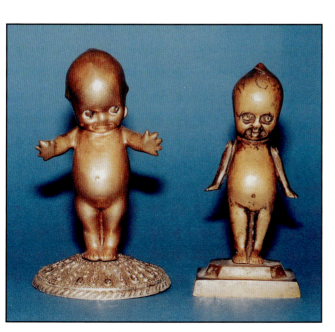

5" brass Kewpie mascot, no wings, added to 3.5" base for car radiator, $800-1000; 5" brass Kewpie paperweight on 2.5" x 1.75" base, $200-400.

4" chrome plated brass Kewpie without wings, poor features, mounted on Model T Ford radiator cap, $100-200; 2.25" Kewpie mounted on dog bone pedal car radiator cap, $100-150; 6.5" pewter Scootles, © Rose O'Neill on feet, $800-1000.

2.5" brass Kewpie, marked Art Brass Co., New York, $100-150; 2.5" painted metal Kewpie nodder, $400-600; 3" brass Kewpie with hands behind back on wood base, $100-200.

3" x 1.75" pewter Kewpie with wings, lying down beside compass, Japan finish, marked made in Japan, $300-400.

Metal chocolate molds, 4.75" Kewpie gal wearing dress, 5.25" mold, marked 16765, 23, $150-200; 4.75" Kewpie without wings, 5.25" mold, marked 16766, TC Weygandt Co, NY, made in Germany, $150-200.

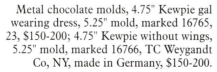

3" tin Kewpie chocolate mold, $20-30; 3" Kewpie paper-weight, Purdue Foundry, $30-50.

13.25" x 10.5" Excelsior Creamery Co. ice cream tray, Kewpie with tennis racket, $800-1000; 13.5" square Schneider's Ice Cream tray, two Kewpies blowing bubbles, $400-600.

13" x 10.5" tray with eleven Kewpies making lemonade, made by H.D. Beach Co., Coshocton, O., $500-700; 13" x 10.5" tray with twelve Kewpies picking blackberries, same marking, $500-700.

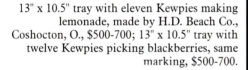

13.5" x 10.5" Crystal Ice Cream tray with baseball Kewpie eating ice cream, $800-1000; 13.5" square Alpha Ice Cream tray with four Kewpies and large strawberry, $600-800.

15.25" x 10.5" Fairmont's Ice Cream tray with Kewpie eating ice cream, tray has red painted border, $400-600; 17.5" x 11.25" Fosselman's Ice Cream tray, Kewpie serving ice cream on a tray, $400-600.

13.5" x 10.5" Sidebottom Ice Cream tray with Kewpie eating ice cream, $600-800; 13.5" square Cortland Ice Cream Co. tray, three Kewpies ready to sample the ice cream, $600-800.

12 oz. Kewpie Pop can, black cherry soda, Mammoth Spring Canning Co., Sussex, WI, $150; 5" Kewpie Kleanser can from Australia, "Cleans everything," $100-125.

1970s Kewpie diced carrots, $30-40; Kewpie can opener, $400-500; 1932 Kewpie beets, $45-65.

3" x 3.5" Uncle Hob and Kewpie pail from 1930s,
$1000-1200; 3" x 3" Kewpie Beach pail, Scootles
Tourist, Kewpie castle, © 1937 by Rose O'Neill,
$700-900; 2.75" x 3.25" not Rose O'Neill but
Kewpie pail, Kewpie riding turtle, $50-100.

Back view of Kewpie sand pails.

7.25" x 10.75" Kewpie drum from 1921, tin lithograph, "The Jolly Kewpie Band" flag, reg. US pat.
off., mark of quality Converse, $5000-6000.

Back view of Kewpie drum.

13.5" x 21" x 8" large Kewpie garter display cabinet, tin lithograph, Kewpies on two sides modeling Kewpie garters, "Don't you want a pair? Kewpie Garter with the Pin that Locks," ten compartments for storage boxes, large Kewpie on top, hinged to lay flat, $3000-3500.

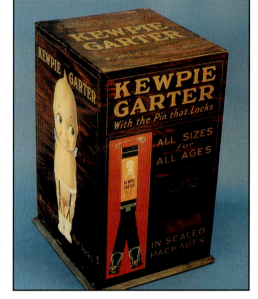

11.5" x 7" x 8" metal Kewpie garter cabinet, tin lithograph, two Kewpies modeling garters pictured on the side of the box, "Do you want a pair? Kewpie Garter with the Pin that Locks," all sizes for all ages, 25¢ in sealed packages, $2000-2500.

Back view of garter cabinet, showing five sizes and color cardboard storage boxes.

Back view of sterling silver Kewpie salt shaker and sterling Kewpie bell showing Paye and Baker (P & B) markings.

4" P & B sterling silver standing Kewpie bells, Trademark Kewpie, $200-400; P & B sterling knife rest, 2.75" x 1.75", $400-500; 1.75" sterling figural kicking Kewpie salt spoon, $125-175; 2" sterling figural standing Kewpie salt spoon, $125-175; 3.5" silver plate salt and pepper shakers, made in Japan, $100-150.

Sterling P & B Kewpie items: 2.5" napkin ring, $300-400; 3" salt and pepper, $300-400; 1.25" x .5" unmarked salt and pepper, applied kicking Kewpie, $300-400; two standing Kewpies at ends of knife rest, 1.75" x 2.75", $400-500; 6.25" Kewpie butter knife, $300-400.

P & B marked sterling utensils: 5.5" relish serving fork, $150-250; 6.25" cake server, $200-300; 5" figural Kewpie fork, $250-350; 5" figural Kewpie spoon, $250-350;, 4.25" spoon with etched scene in bowl, Kewpies Taking Baby to the Circus (foreground), $400-500; 4" fork, $200-300; 4.25" spoon, $200-300; 5" knife, $300-400.

1.25" Kewpie knife holder, P & B sterling, $400-500; 5" youth fork with 2" Kewpie, P & B sterling, Trademark Kewpie, $250-350; 4.25" fork with 1.5" Kewpie, P & B sterling, Trademark Kewpie, $200-300.

Sterling Kewpie baby pusher, 2" wide with 2.5" handle, marked P & B, $500-700; 4.25" sterling baby Kewpie spoon, marked P & B, $200-300.

9" bronze Kewpie topped letter opener, $150-200.

Reverse side of letter opener with likeness of Rose O'Neill.

6.25" ring and stick pin holder with 1.5" Kewpie marked Rd633819, +*EP*+ on base, $200-300.

Kewpie Kids ring, P & B, Trademark Kewpie, $150-250; QT kids ring, no marks, $50-100; cloisonné Kewpie on sterling ring, P & B, Trademark Kewpie, $250-350; sterling Thinker, P & B, ©, Trademark Kewpie, $200-300; sterling kicking, P & B, Trademark Kewpie, ©, $150-250; standing Kewpie, no marks, $50-100; 5.25" sterling watch fob with 1.25" sterling Trademark Kewpie, ©, Kewpie probably added to fob, $350-450; 7" sterling P & B bib holder with kicking Kewpies, $300-400; 1" gold plated Kewpie necklace, no marks, $50-100; 1" undetermined material Kewpie necklace, made in Germany, Albert H Oechsle, Jefferson City, MO, $75-100; 6.5" grosgrain ribbon watch fob, 1" cloisonné Kewpie cook, CMC, sterling, Trademark, ©, $400-500; 7.75" grosgrain ribbon watch fob, 1.25" 10K gold, Trademark Kewpie, ©, watch fob attached to pin holder, $400-500.

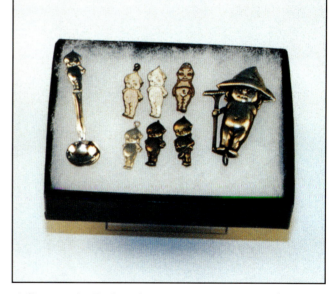

2.5" spoon pin, Trademark Kewpie, P & B, Sheffield, $200-300; 1" standing charm, Trademark Kewpie, $100-200; 1" standing cloisonné charm, sterling, P & B, Trademark Kewpie, ©, $150-250; standing pin, CMC, Trademark Kewpie, ©, $150-250; 1" standing cloisonné pin, P & B, sterling, Trademark Kewpie, ©, $150-250; Kewpie Cook pin, CMC, Trademark Kewpie, ©, $150-250; 1" Soldier pin, lost his cloisonné, sterling, P & B, Trademark Kewpie, ©, $150-250; 2" brass Truart sterling Gardener pin with ring for adding charms, $100-200.

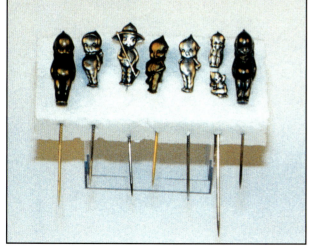

Beauty pins: 1.25" gold plated standing, Trademark Kewpie, ©, $250-350; 1" Careful of His Voice, silver plated, CMC, Trademark Kewpie, ©, $200-300; 1" Gardener, silver plated, CMC, Trademark Kewpie, ©, $200-300; 1" Cook, gold plated, CMC, Trademark Kewpie, ©, $200-300; standing Trademark Kewpie, CMC, ©, $200-300; .75" Thinker, P & B, sterling, Trademark Kewpie, ©, $175-275; .5" kicker, P & B, sterling, Trademark Kewpie, ©, $175-275; 1.25" sterling standing, Trademark Kewpie, ©, $250-300.

.5" sterling P & B kicking Kewpie hat pin, $200-250; .75" gold P & B Thinker hatpin, $200-250; 1" sterling figural Thinker and 1" gold figural Thinker hatpins on original presentation card, "Kewpies - The Little Happy Gods, They drive away your troubles," Trademark Kewpie, ©, $450-550; 1.25" sterling standing Kewpie hatpin, Trademark, $200-250; 1" cloisonné Kewpie Gardener hatpin, CMC, sterling, Trademark, ©, $200-250.

2" brass Kewpie on 1.25" whistle, $150-200; 1.25" Kewpie on 9" hatpin, marked Kewpie on front and Rose O'Neill on back, $200-250; 2.5" pewter Kewpie on heart base, 11" chain with 3" pencil, $200-300.

1" Cracker Jack plastic Kewpie, Japan, $25-35; 1.25" clear resin Trademark Kewpie, $100-200; 1.25" sterling Trademark Kewpie, © on feet, $200-300; .5" sterling kicking P & B Kewpie charm, Trademark, ©, $75-175; .5" 10K gold kicking P & B Kewpie, $100-200; .75" sterling Thinker charm, $50-100; ivory Kewpie, no marks, $100-200; 1" Cracker Jack plastic Kewpie charm, Japan, $25-35; 1.5" marked on base, Kewpie, Rose O'Neill, made in Germany, Albert H Oechsle, Jefferson City, MO, $50-100; 1.25" pink painted resin Trademark Kewpie, $100-200; 1" resin Kewpie, no marks, $25-35.

1.25" Kewpie on 5" hatpin, P & B, 10K gold, on original presentation card, $500-600.

1" resin painted, flesh tone Kewpie, embossed Trademark Kewpie on back, $50-75; 1" cloisonné standing Kewpie, P & B, three hearts, sterling, Trademark, ©, $150-200; 1" gold Kewpie, leaf indentation on chest, $125-150.

Chapter Four

Miscellaneous Kewpie Items

Shown here are a variety of additional Kewpie items. The ceramic Kewpie salt and pepper shakers were made for each holiday. German-made, these are as beautiful as the bisque German Kewpies. During World War I, new suppliers for Kewpie products were sought by Rose. Celluloid Kewpies from Japan filled some of the void. Molds for the Thinker and standing Kewpie with fixed and moveable arms were sold to carnivals. The carnival workers would then make chalk Kewpies as needed. These prizes were given to winners of midway games. The Kewpie statuette made of wood pulp composition was manufactured by the Tip Top Toy Co. in 1917 and sold six dozen per case for carnival prizes.

With the creation of the Cuddle Kewpie in 1925, Rose assigned this patent to her sister, Callista. Callista designed the first patterns and hand made the Cuddle Kewpies to sell in their Saugatuck, Connecticut shop. The Cuddle Kewpies were made of satin, cotton, silk jersey, or plush. The faces were printed cloth pressed into shape with a stiff underlining. These Cuddle Kewpies had individual fingers but as the Kewpies became more mass produced, they lost their fingers to a mitten-like hand. Callista set up a cottage business with seamstresses to make these Kewpies. K&K Toy Company of New York City, a subsidiary of the George F. Borgfeldt & Company, were the earliest makers of the Cuddle Kewpie. In 1929, King Innovations Inc. began manufacturing the Cuddle Kewpies. From 1935 to 1952, Krueger Co., N.Y., held the contract. Later, Knickerbocker Toy Company Inc. produced these cuddly soft Kewpies. K&K, King Innovations, and Krueger all used the silk Kewpie mask face while Knickerbocker used vinyl faces and heads on plush Kewpie bodies.

Sears Roebuck and Company introduced a Kewpie Kamera on August 24, 1915. As this had not been authorized by either Rose or the Borgfeldt Company, Rose sued them. The judge ruled against Sears Roebuck in that the artwork was copyrighted. Sears was allowed to continue using the Kewpie name on the camera, however, because Rose did not have the name trademarked for cameras. If you have one of the early Sears Roebuck and Company Kewpie Kameras with the Kewpie drawings on the box, it is more valuable than the boxed Kewpie Kameras shown in this chapter.

In 1935, Rose created the Scootles dolls, the Baby Tourist from her Kewpieville illustrations. You can tell the very earliest composition Scootles by the shelf at the back of the neck on which the head rests. The later Scootles, produced by the Cameo Doll Company, used the Kewpie bodies and legs but the more muscular Scootles arms.

With the creation of the Ho-Ho in 1940, Rose and Callista hoped to recoup some of their fortune. As noted earlier, however, Rose's timing was off with this creation: a Buddha looking figurine was not a popular item given the bombing of Pearl Harbor. They produced the Ho-Ho at their home, Bonniebrook, and most were given away to friends. In the late 1940s, Richard O'Neill (son of John Hugh, Rose's older brother), using the original rubber molds, had one thousand 5.5" Ho-Hos cast. He then contracted with the Republic, Missouri, high school art class to have these Ho-Hos air brushed and their features painted. They can be found as Caucasians and Blacks, dressed in red, green, yellow, blue, pink, and black. These Ho-Hos were sold at the Shepherd of the Hills gift shop in Branson, Missouri.

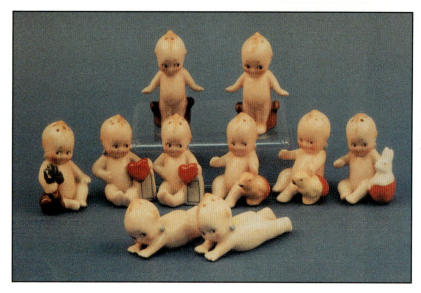

Kewpie salt and pepper shakers, 1.25" x 2.5" Kewpies on tummies; 2" shamrock shaker; 2" Valentine; 2" Easter Kewpie with chick in egg; 2" Easter Kewpie with rabbit in egg; all $400-600 a set; 2.5" standing Kewpie with stump, $300-500 a set.

2.75" glazed Kewpie salt and pepper shakers with turkey, $600-800 a set; 2.75" Kewpie with gray rabbit, $500-700 a set.

2" Kewpie with gray rabbit salt shaker, $200-300; 2" Easter Kewpie with yellow chick at side, $200-300; 2" Easter Kewpie with rabbit in egg salt and pepper shakers, $400-600 a set.

2.75" glazed salt shaker with chick, round patent sticker on back, $400-600; 2.75" glazed salt shaker Kewpie holding pumpkin, round patent sticker on back, $400-600.

2.25" seated Kewpie salt and pepper shakers, made in Japan, $75-100 a set; 2" Kewpies with hands under chin, made in Japan, $50-75 a set; 2.25" Kewpies with hands under chin, $50-75 a set.

4.75" celluloid straight-legged talcum shaker Kewpie, jointed arms, marked 4/0 with original cork plug, $300-500.

4.75" back view of previous celluloid talcum shaker Kewpie, raised 4/0 on back, $300-500; 5" Coca Cola advertisement, Merry Christmas - Coca-Cola, 6 oz. bottle cap hat, made in occupied Japan, $300-500; 3.25" straight-legged celluloid figure, Kewpie Germany heart sticker, marked 8/0, $75-150; 6" straight-legged celluloid figure, © Rose O'Neill circle sticker on back, $150-250.

8.5" crepe paper dressed celluloid Kewpie with wings, Kewpie heart sticker, $200-300; 13.5" straight-legged celluloid Kewpie with jointed arms, marking between wings, circle Nippon, $200-300.

139

5.25" dressed Kewpie, marked between wings, pearl tiara on mohair wig, $150-250.

4" celluloid Kewpie, molded trousers and jacket, very expressive face, $100-150; 5" celluloid Kewpie, molded pink hat and skirt, also came in green, circa 1920, $150-200.

Jointed arms celluloid chicken Kewpie in nest, two "I Have a Chicken in France" buttons, $100-150.

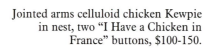

Rubber Kewpies, 3.5" with rubber molded shoes, moveable arms, $200-300; 5.5" standing Kewpie, moveable arms, circa 1913, $300-400.

2.5" rigid armed Kewpie, unknown material, looks like hardened rubber, $100-150.

24" flex-o Kewpie, moveable head, head and body composition, wooden jointed arms and legs, $4000-6000.

32" black display Kewpie on round base, chalk, painted heart on chest, $800-1000.

32" advertising chalk Kewpie, indented heart on base, circa 1914, $600-800; 32" papier mâché Kewpie Twins Shoes for Children advertising Kewpie, paper crown label, Old King Cole Co., Canton, OH USA, $800-1000.

14.5" plaster seated Kewpie, possibly a store display, $300-400.

Brown composition Kewpie Thinkers, made in Italy, circa 1960s, oval red paper label, 9" Thinker with silver Gimbels label, No. 127 in pencil on red label, $200-300; 5.5" Thinker, No. 725 on red label, $100-200; 3.75" Thinker, No. 254 on red label, $50-100.

Composition Kewpie molded in pumpkin candy container, 4.5" x 2.75", Kewpie heart sticker, extremely rare, $800-1000.

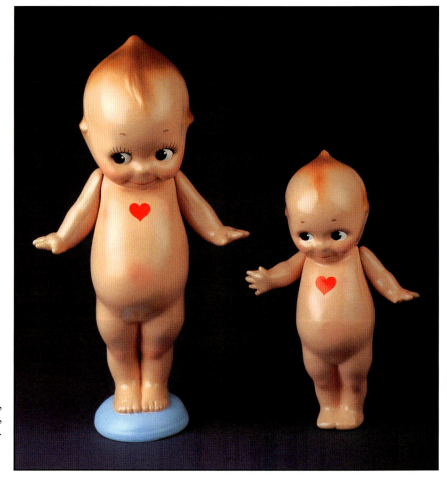

13" composition Kewpie on blue base, jointed arms, painted red heart, $150-250; 9" composition Kewpie, jointed arms, $100-200.

8" composition Kewpie dressed in skirt, original box, jointed arms, heart sticker, rare size, design and copyright Rose O'Neill, Cameo Doll Co., circa 1944, $300-500; 11.5" composition Kewpie, jointed arms, heart sticker, Cameo Doll Co., original box, $200-400; 11.5" composition Black Kewpie, jointed arms, heart sticker, $150-250

8" composition Kewpie with natural hair wig, jointed arms, heart sticker, $150-250.

7.25" chalk carnival saluting Kewpie on 2" base, $100-200; 7" composition Kewpie, jointed arms, $75-150.

12" composition Kewpie in original box, jointed arms and legs, Cameo Doll Co., No. 9713, $400-600.

22" composition head Kewpie with cloth body, doll on left wearing original dress tagged Trademark Kewpie, Reg. US Patent Office, Rose O'Neill, patented March 4, 1913, $1000-1200; second doll with reproduction dress, $800-900.

20" composition head Kewpie with cloth body, composition hands, $1000-1200.

12" premium composition head and half arms Kewpie with cloth body, original tag reads: Kewpie REG US PAT OFF, 1913, R O'NEILL, DES PAT MARCH 4, 1913, $800-1000.

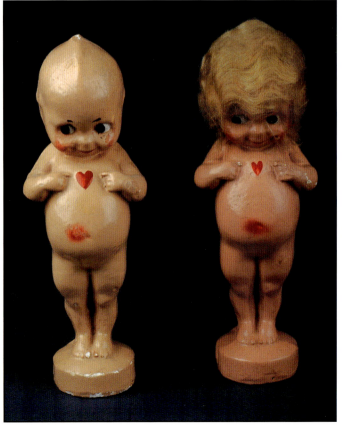

8.5" chalk carnival Kewpie, painted heart, $100-200; 8.5" chalk carnival Kewpie with hair wig, painted heart, $100-200.

13.5" chalk Sailor Kewpie, saluting, circa 1920, $100-200; 13" painted chalk carnival Kewpie, crepe paper dress, jointed arms, raised molded heart, $100-150; 13" chalk carnival Kewpie, feathered costume, jointed arms, $100-150.

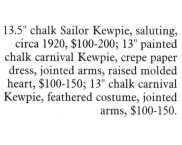

17" lamp with 11" composition Kewpie on 3.25" base, jointed arms, cord comes out center of its back, $300-400; 19" lamp with 12" chalk Kewpie on 5.5" base, human hair wig, silk collar, skirt, and shade, $200-300; 17" lamp with 12" chalk Kewpie, 4.5" base, jointed arms, screw in plug, $100-200.

6" Kewpie Thinker, incised lower back patent des. and copyright, 1913, $200-300; 6" carite Kewpie Thinker, brass button in bottom, patented and copyrighted, 1913, $100-200; 6.25" chalk carnival Kewpie, painted features, $50-75.

6" carite Kewpie Thinker with brass button on bottom, patented & copyrighted - 1913, $100-200.

Three Kewpie Thinkers, $200-300; $150-200; $100-150.

Markings on the three previous Kewpie Thinkers: marked patent copyright on the lower back of the first Thinker; © paper sticker, Kewpie reg. US pat. off., Rose O'Neill, 1913, des. pat. Jul 4 1913; Kewpie paper label, reg U.S. pat. off., des. pat. July, 22, 1913.

Rare 23" early Cuddle Kewpie with fingers, lace collar, $1200-1400.

18.5" Arabella Cuddle Kewpie, original clothes as shown in the Fels Naptha soap ads, 1928, $1400-1600.

10" yellow satin Cuddle Kewpie with lace collar, blue and white flowers printed on ribbon at neck, original box, Krueger N.Y.C., made in USA, $1000-1200.

8" red and white checked, dressed Cuddle Kewpie, King Innovations, © Rose O'Neill, $2200-2500.

14" pink jersey Cuddle Kewpie, original box, $600-800; 10" yellow satin Cuddle Kewpie, same as previous picture, $1000-1200; 11" red jersey Cuddle Kewpie, original tag, white ribbon, original box, marked "K" traditional quality, Krueger, N.Y.C., $500-700.

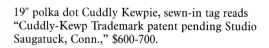

19" polka dot Cuddly Kewpie, sewn-in tag reads "Cuddly-Kewp Trademark patent pending Studio Saugatuck, Conn.," $600-700.

16" plush Cuddle Kewpie, zippered opening in back, tagged Trademark Kewpie, King Innovations, $600-700.

22" well loved jersey knit fabric Kewpie, $200-300; 18" salmon-colored jersey knit fabric Kewpie, tagged King Inv., $500-600; 12.5" blue jersey knit Kewpie, Krueger, $200-300; 10.5" red jersey knit Kewpie, no tag but a Krueger, $150-250; 8" salmon jersey knit, King Inv., $400-500.

14" Cuddle Kewpie, red silk, made by Callista, $600-800; 14" maroon velvet, handmade in Westport, Conn., Callista organized cottage work force, $600-800; 15" salmon jersey Cuddle Kewpie, $350-450.

Red jersey Cuddle Kewpie, original red ribbon, $250-350.

19" Kewpie has half body, red and white taffeta pajamas, sewn-in ribbon attached to head for hanging, she has lost her maid's doily hat, manufactured by Krueger N.Y.C., $600-800.

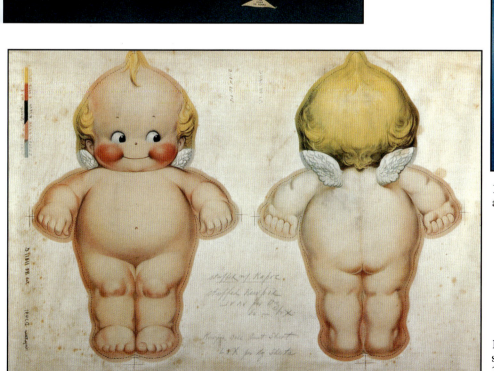

Pair of 11.75" red jersey Kewpie faced dolls, satin tag reads "Krueger N.Y.C.," Blue Ribbon Creation paper tag, no wings or topknot, stuffed with foam rubber, possibly made after contract with Rose expired, $200-400.

10.5" pink plush doll with Kewpie face, hair added, Krueger label, $200-300.

17" x 11.5" printed cloth Kewpie to be stuffed with kapok, overall size is 20" x 28.5", $150-250.

24" x 18" linen embroidered pillow top, nine Kewpies holding an American flag, American Kewpies, No. 5787 Royal Society Celesta, © 1913, Rose O'Neill, $400-500.

Boxed baby Kewpie garter and diaper holders, member of Kewpie garter family, FRANCONIA, $600-800.

6.25" green Kewpie hankie box, also in red, marked No. 2606 Kewpie Hankie 1/4 doz., with Kewpie hankies, $300-400; 6" box shows Kewpie Cook feeding a rabbit with other animal characters, one hankie, $200-300; 10.5" square Kewpie hankies, $50-100 each.

8.75 x 4.5" Kewpie hankie box, 8.25" silk hankie with blue border, marked © ROW, same artwork as Help Wanted Klever Kard, $200-300. The Help Wanted Klever Kard is a postcard produced by the Campbell Art Co. in 1914. The Klever Kards are die cut to fold and make an easel stand up card.

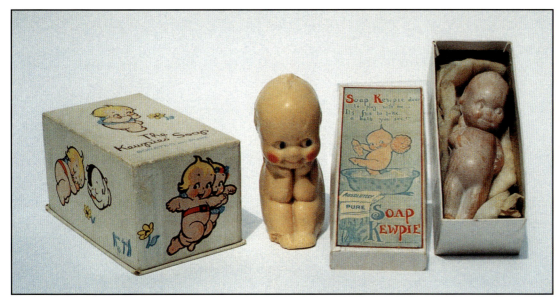

3.75" Kewpie Thinker soap in 2.75" x 2.5" x 4.5" box, soap incised Rose O'Neill Kewpie by Shulton, 1935, © Rose O'Neill, $150-250; 4" straight-legged Kewpie soap, incised in a heart on back Kewpie reg. US pat off, US DES OFF 4368C, © 1917, Rose O'Neill Wilson, 2" x 1.75" x 4.75" box reads, "Soap Kewpie dear to play with me. It's fun to take a bath, you see!" Absolutely Pure, signed O'Neill, $150-250.

4" blown glass Kewpie with clown ruffled collar and clown hat, $150-250.

3.25" glass Kewpie candy container bank with slotted metal lid, 1.75" x 1.75" bank, $200-400.

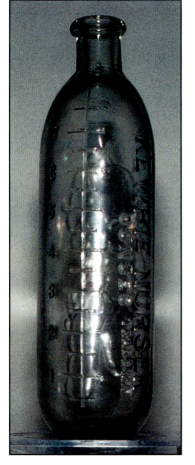

7" glass Kewpie nurser bottle, embossed Kewpie with bottle in mouth, $1200-1400.

Bottom of glass nurser bottle, reads Rose O'Neill © 1919.

Kewpie Kameras with boxes: 6.5" x 7" x 5" size 3A camera, $75-125 without box, $200-250 with box; 4" x 5.5" x 3.5" size 2 camera, $50-75 without box, $150-200 with box.

Lantern and Kewpie slides, 1913, magic lantern not O'Neill with kerosene lamp inside with lens to magnify, 1" x 4.5" slides of different action Kewpie characters in 1.5" x 5" box reads "New Kewpie Magic Lantern Slides," "Original Design by Rose O'Neill," $300-400; 1.5" x 6" slides, $100 each.

White unpainted bisque Kewpie attached to clock, 4.75" x 4.75" x 1.75", marked with a crown and eight-sided star, 9923, $2500-3000.

23" wooden ice cream freezer bucket, 16" Kewpie painted on side is wearing top hat and monocle and ready to dish up a bowl, $1200-1500.

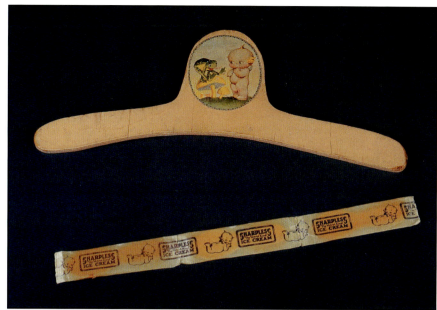

11" x 4" Kewpie clothes hanger with 3" Kewpie and frog decal, $75-100; three wooden Sharpless ice cream spoons, Kewpie pictured laying on stomach, $20 each.

Two Kewpie toothbrushes in box, Coronet Brush Company, Osaka, Japan, $400-600.

9" x 4" Austria glass pedestal candy jar with gold trim, flower garland draped with gold bows, three embossed painted Kewpies, $150-250.

Assortment of Kewpie advertising items from the Mammoth Springs Canning Company, Sussex, Wisconsin: pen and pencils, $20-30 each; matches, $5-10 each; cigarette lighter with box, $75-100.

18" x 12" paper advertising poster for "True Fruit" soda by Rose O'Neill, The Happy Kids, J. Hungerford Smith Co., Rochester, NY, $300-400.

Framed Kewpie canned vegetable labels used by Mammoth Spring Canning Co. from 1925 to 1932, $45-65 each.

28" x 18" paper advertising poster for Kewpie Golden Corn, Mammoth Spring Canning Co., Sussex, WI, $100-150.

3.5" x 4.75" silk Kewpie purse, $150-200; 4.5" x 3.75" leather "Marketing" purse, Careful of His Voice with umbrella, $100-150.

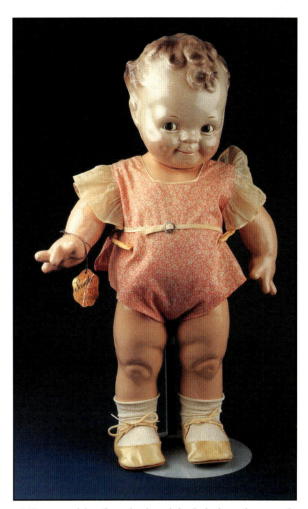

21" composition Scootles in original clothes, shoes, and hang tag, jointed arms and legs, design and copyright by Rose O'Neill, m'f'd's, Cameo Doll Co., Port Allegany, PA., $1000-1200.

13.5" sleepy-eyed composition Scootles, original clothes, jointed arms and legs, $800-900; 12" composition sleepy-eyed Scootles, original clothes with Scootles tag on dress, $800-900; 15" sleepy-eyed composition Scootles, original clothes, $900-1000.

21" sleepy-eyed Scootles, original dress. This doll was purchased for the Bonniebrook Historical Society at the Butterfield Auction of Shepherd of the Hills Farm Rose O'Neill collection. It was featured on one of the Shepherd of the Hills postcards, $1200-1500.

12" composition Scootles in original sunsuit, hang tag, jointed arms and legs, $300-400; 8" Scootles in original sunsuit, jointed arms and legs, $500-700.

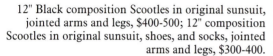

12" Black composition Scootles in original sunsuit, jointed arms and legs, $400-500; 12" composition Scootles in original sunsuit, shoes, and socks, jointed arms and legs, $300-400.

8" bisque Scootles, stamped Germany, incised Scootles and © Rose O'Neill on feet, $600-800.

18" cloth molded face Scootles with yarn hair, original clothes, shoes, and socks, original box, Scootles, A Character Doll by Rose O'Neill, Manufactured by Richard G. Krueger, Inc., New York, NY, patent applied for, circa 1935, $2200-2500.

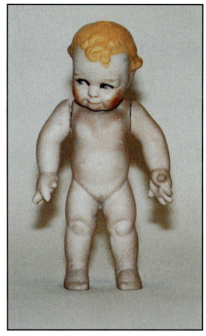

6.5" bisque Scootles, incised Scootles, © Rose O'Neill on feet, stamped Japan, $300-500.

4" celluloid bride in net skirt and train, Kewpie Doll box, $125-175; 5.5" original bisque Scootles in box, incised Scootles and © Rose O'Neill on feet, shield Scootles sticker, made in Germany, $400-600; 5.5" bisque Scootles, incised Scootles and © Rose O'Neill on feet, shield Scootles sticker, made in Germany, without box, $200-300.

8" bisque Scootles, incised Scootles and © Rose O'Neill on feet, dressed in a Scootles' labeled dress and panties, $700-900.

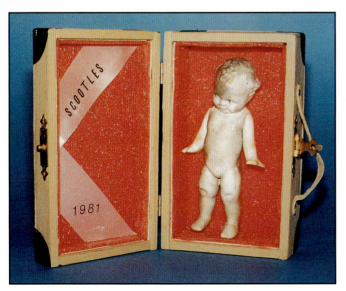

5.5" bisque Scootles with Kewpie arms found in the ashes of Bonniebrook.

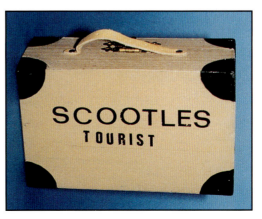

Scootles Tourist case.

9" Ho-Ho with candle holder base, incised Rose O'Neill copyright 1940, $400-600; 6.5" Ho-Ho with black candle holder base, incised Rose O'Neill copyright 1940, painted plaster of Paris, $300-500.

5.5" Bonniebrook Ho-Ho, trademark, plaster of Paris, $200-300; 5" Ho-Ho candle holder dime bank, 6.25" x 6.75" x 3.5" overall, Rose O'Neill copyright, $300-400; 5.5" pink Ho-Ho, incised Ho-Ho on back, © Rose O'Neill, 1940, $100-200.

5.5" Black plaster of Paris Ho-Ho, embossed Ho-Ho on back, Rose O'Neill copyright 1940, $100-200; 5.5" yellow plaster of Paris Ho-Ho, embossed Ho-Ho on back, Rose O'Neill copyright 1940, $100-200.

5.5" pink Ho-Ho, incised Ho-Ho on back, © Rose O'Neill, 1940, $100-200; 5.5" Black Ho-Ho, incised Ho-Ho on back, © Rose O'Neill, 1940, $150-250; Bonniebrook Ho-Ho gift from Rose and Callista, trademark, Rose O'Neill, shellac finish, $300-400.

Bottom view of Bonniebrook Ho-Ho gift from Rose and Callista, incised on bottom. This Ho-Ho has a shellac finish over plaster of Paris, $300-400.

Made at Bonniebrook Ho-Ho for Lillian Short by Rose O'Neill, shellac finish over plaster of Paris, $300-400.

6.25" x 7" replicas of Jasperware pieces, made and marketed by Shepherd of the Hills Farm, $50-75 each.

159

Bibliography

Banneck, Janet A. *The Antique Postcards of Rose O'Neill*. Revised and Illustrated by Susan Brown Nicholson. Lisle, Illinois: Greater Chicago Productions, 1992.

Edward, Linda. "End Of An Era." *Doll Reader*, February, 2002.

Gillett, Luther, and Karen L. Stewart. "Ho-Ho The Little Laughing Buddha." *Kewpiesta Kourier*, Fall, 1995.

Gillett, Luther, and Karen Stewart. "Kewpie Jasperware Update." *Kewpiesta Kourier*, Winter, 1992.

Gillett, Luther, and Karen Stewart. "Marching Orders." *Kewpiesta Kourier Newsletter*, 1998.

Horine, Maude M. *Memories of Rose O'Neill*. Branson, Missouri: Maude M. Horine, 1950; Revised edition, 1954.

Kelly, Cleo. *The Kewpies in My Life*. Tulsa, Oklahoma: Kelly's Enterprises, 1973.

Leuzzi, Marlene, and Robert J. Kershner. *Kewpies In Action*. Englewood, Colorado, 1971.

Lyndhurst, Joe. *Military Collectibles*. Salamander Books, Random House, 1983.

O'Neill, Rose. *Cordially yours, Rose O'Neill*. Compiled by Barbara (Trimble) Abernathy and Mary H. Trimble, 1968.

O'Neill, Rose. *The Story of Rose O'Neill, An Autobiography*. Edited with Introduction by Miriam Formanek-Brunell. Columbia, Missouri: University of Missouri Press, 1997.

O'Neill, Rose. *Scrapbook of Early Illustrations by Rose O'Neill*. Compiled by David O'Neill, 1999.

O'Neill, Rose. *Rose Cecil O'Neill (1874-1944)*. Unpublished Memoirs.

Ruggles, Rowena Godding. *The One Rose*. Oakland, California: Rowena Godding Ruggles, 1964; 2nd Ed. and Supplement, 1972.

The Drawings and Illustrations of Rose Cecil O'Neill Catalogue. Springfield Art Museum and the Missouri Arts Council, 1989.